THE
GODS OF REVOLUTION

CHRISTOPHER DAWSON

The
Gods of Revolution

Introduction by Arnold Toynbee

Appreciation by James Oliver

SIDGWICK & JACKSON
LONDON

ISBN 0 283 97820 1

Printed in Great Britain by
The Garden City Press Limited,
Letchworth, Hertfordshire, for
Sidgwick and Jackson Limited
1 Tavistock Chambers, Bloomsbury Way
London W.C.1

CONTENTS

ACKNOWLEDGEMENTS

This work of Christopher Dawson's has never been published in book form but some of the chapters were published in various periodicals in the U.S.A. some years ago. Grateful acknowledgement is made therefore to the Editors of *The Review of Politics*, *The South Atlantic Quarterly*, *The Catholic World*, and *The Four Quarters* for permission to use here material which first appeared in their pages.

I should like to express my thanks to Dr Arnold Toynbee for his masterly Introduction to this book; to Mr James Oliver for his Appreciation and for his kindness in undertaking the index and bibliography; and to Mr E. I. Watkin for much helpful advice. Last, but by no means least, I should like to thank Mr John J. Mulloy of Philadelphia for his valuable work in editing and collating the original manuscript some ten years ago when my father held the Stillman Professorship of Roman Catholic Studies at Harvard University.

CHRISTINA SCOTT
(Literary Executor)

Tunbridge Wells
Kent

INTRODUCTION

Christopher Dawson's virtues have become familiar to readers of his books published in his lifetime. In the present book, these virtues make themselves manifest again. Dawson's work has always been both original and sincere. His thoughts and feelings are always his own. They are never taken by him at second hand, and this quality makes his treatment of a subject rewarding. However often the particular subject may have been dealt with by his predecessors, Dawson's handling throws new light on it. Originality and sincerity do not always go together. There are writers who strain after novelty self-consciously. Dawson tells his readers straightforwardly what he truly feels and thinks. His religion, and his views of life and of history, are definite. At the same time, he has a sympathetic understanding for people whose outlooks differ from his own. A case in point is his exposition of Robespierre's religion in this book.

The book is in three parts. Part One explores the French Revolution's apparently innocuous academic antecedents. The middle part deals with the awful consequences of theories translated into action. Part Three is concerned with the Revolution's aftermath. This last part inevitably ends with a question-mark; for the impact of the Revolution is still continuing in our day. Dawson puts the question in terms of his own beliefs. For him, religion is the most important thing in life, and the destiny of the western civilization is bound up with Christianity. If western civilization were to become irretrievably 'post-Christian', its prospects, in Dawson's view, would be dark. He notes, with a sense of relief, that the first reaction to the Revolu-

tion was a revulsion towards Christianity, but his insight
and his frankness do not let him assume that this is the
last word in the story. In his eyes, the fateful question is
still an open one.

Since religion holds the central place in Dawson's view,
he looks at the French Revolution primarily, though not
at all exclusively, in its religious aspect, and this is the
original feature of the account of the Revolution in the
present book. In the Revolution, a sinister ancient religion
which had been dormant suddenly re-erupted with
elemental violence. This revenant was the fanatical worship
of collective human power. The Terror was only the first
of the mass-crimes that have been committed during the
last hundred and seventy years in this evil religion's name.

Dawson brings out the French Revolution's extraordinary paradoxes. Robespierre was a disinterested idealist.
His humanitarianism led him into sponsoring the Terror.
His enthusiasm for reason led him into the most irrational
form of religion. Humanity is a ludicrous object for human
beings to worship. In Robespierre's naïve formulation of it,
this resuscitated man-worship was ephemeral; but the
reality that underlay the pedantic Robespierre-ian forms
has continued to govern our lives, and holocausts have been
sacrificed to it by generations which wanted, not self-
sacrifice, but fleshpots.

The Revolution was political, not social. It was a
victorious assertion of the supremacy of the *bourgeoisie*.
In the 1790s, as in 1848 and 1871, the proletariat was
crushed as soon as it tried to become the *bourgeoisie*'s com-
petitor, instead of remaining its tool and its dupe. In the
1790s, the cause for social revolution was championed, not
by the anti-clericals, but by a Catholic priest, Jacques
Roux, working in a Parisian slum parish. He was a precursor
of the French 'working priests' of the twentieth century,
and he was denounced in the Convention as being all of a
piece with the rural priests who were leading the peasant
revolt in La Vendée. Father Roux and his Vendean con-
frères were, in truth, counter-revolutionaries if the
Revolution boils down to the creation of massive new vested

interests. While the idéologues and the Terrorists occupied the foreground of the stage, the background gave ample room for people whose main concern was not either theories or massacres, but the sly acquisition of real estate on advantageous terms. These material results of the Revolution were confirmed by the termination of the Terror, and they survived the Empire and the Restoration.

The urban proletariat, which had been used by the *bourgeois* revolutionaries as a battering ram, gained none of the spoils. On the other hand, the peasantry, who had been the Revolution's formidable, though politically unsuccessful, opponents, shared the economic spoils of the Revolution with the nouveaux riches members of the *bourgeoisie*.

The Revolution's supreme paradox was that, in the act of deposing the traditional Christian 'Establishment', it opened the way for an atavistic return to a pre-Christian religion: the worship of collective human power which had been the religion of the pagan Roman Empire and of the Greek city-states which the Roman Empire had incorporated. This worship of human power is about ninety per cent of the religion of about ninety per cent of the present generation of mankind. Shall we succeed in shaking it off? And, if we remain enslaved to it, whither will it lead us? This is the biggest of the many questions that are raised in the present book. The book is of the same high standard as the author's previous works.

ARNOLD TOYNBEE

CHRISTOPHER DAWSON:

An Appreciation

by James Oliver

A writer who makes an impact on the educated opinion of his age acquires in time a reputation very different from that which first marked his name. It is impossible now to recapture the shock of *Childe Harold's Pilgrimage* – or of Eliot's *Waste Land* more than a generation ago. T. S. Eliot, O.M. is a very different figure from the delight of students or the horror of their teachers in the 1920s. Eliot was a great admirer of Christopher Dawson, whose *Progress and Religion* first appeared in 1929, some ten years before Eliot's *Idea of a Christian Society*. As critics, both first resisted, then altered, a current of thought.

Progress and Religion was a surprising, even a shocking work, but what caused the greatest surprise was the depth and serenity of its scholarship. People almost expect, even hope, to be surprised by a poet: from a scholar they more often await facts than judgements, but *Progress and Religion* was a judgement of their accepted ideas weighted with hard facts.

Spengler's *Decline of the West* had appeared in English in the 1920s, but its pessimism was regarded as an expression of Germany's defeat, and the British no longer had the confidence of their fathers in German philosophy: Spengler was too close to Schopenhauer for an age which still had faith in the League of Nations, after a war which had ended war. Yet here was Dawson, an Englishman and an Oxford scholar, calmly pointing out that their belief in progress was a religion which dated from the eighteenth century. And he went further than that: he even sympathized with this religion, as with every idea which has raised the human spirit. This early ecumenicity surprised readers even more. Brought up on Frazer's *Golden Bough,* they were used to comparative religion, but all their comparisons were odious, for they assumed that to explain religion was to discredit it.

Dawson, on the contrary, explained religion as the soul of a culture, which became secular or political only in decline, and he was able to show the origins of progress in deism and pietism. Belief in progress was the motive of French rationalism, German idealism, English liberalism, and it arose within a Christian culture and was unlikely to survive it.

The proof of this is that contemporary pessimism has turned with relief even to the apocalyptic Omega visions of a Teilhard de Chardin, to renew its faith in progress as a substitute for religion. Christopher Dawson would no doubt have respected even that, for he was uniquely generous to sincere motives, as he showed in his treatment of Wells's *Outline of History,* so harshly attacked by Belloc. Dawson came as a great relief to the generation after Belloc, exhausted by brutal polemics and insensitive dismissals of unchristened but honest motives.

Yet Dawson himself was a stronger champion of Christian culture, to which most of his later works are devoted. He had been early disturbed by the strange partiality of those scholars, especially in Britain and North America, who would concede, even insist on, the overwhelming importance of Islam, Hinduism, Buddhism to other cultures, but ignore or dismiss as a special study Christianity in relation to their own culture.

To Dawson this appeared an inability to regard a culture with detachment. In fact the British between the wars were singularly unaware of their own convictions, of their deep attachment to progress and liberalism: unaware even of their strong nationalism, which they considered a disease peculiar to the Italians and Germans.

Yet these British convictions had been shaken by the First World War, and a leading publicist, Dean Inge, recommended *Progress and Religion* to them as 'one of the great books of our time'. So they learnt, as Paul Valéry was to say in the Second World War, that 'civilizations are mortal'. Dean Inge was noted for his pessimism, but no mood of that sort troubled Dawson's serenity, as he disclosed to Christians, sunk in bourgeois prosperity, the real treasures of their culture. His later works, from *The Making of Europe,* 1932, to his Harvard lectures on *Christendom* 1965-7, were all directed towards the recovery of that culture.

These works on culture led some historians to regard him with the suspicion they gave to Spengler and Arnold Toynbee as exponents of metahistory. In an answer to Alan Bullock's attack on metahistory Dawson wrote:

'The academic historian is perfectly right in insisting on the importance of the techniques of historical criticism and research. But the mastery of these techniques will not produce great history, any more than a mastery of metrical technique will produce great poetry. For this something more is necessary . . . The experience of the great historians such as Tocqueville and Ranke leads me to believe that a universal metahistorical vision . . . partaking more of the nature of religious contemplation than of scientific generalisation lies very close to the sources of their creative power.' – *The Problem of Metahistory,* 1951.

In writing this Dawson was not defending himself, nor was metahistory his greatest gift. Those works of his on culture drew their importance from his unique gift as a historian of ideas, first revealed in *Progress and Religion.*

So it is just that his last and posthumous work, *The Gods of Revolution,* should return to a brilliant analysis of ideas on revolution and particularly on the French Revolution. Here again academic historians rightly insist on recent research, especially in economic and local history. Dawson was too faithful to Le Play not to admit Place, Work, People as primary constituents of social life. He had written:

'It is the besetting sin of the idealist to sacrifice reality to his ideals; to reject life because it fails to come up to his ideals;

and this vice is just as prevalent among religious idealists as secular ones.' – *Cultural Polarity and Religious Schism, 1942.*

Yet he always insisted that even the most primitive culture was 'never a mere passive result of material forces. The human factor is always active and creative.' Instancing Bushmen hunters of South Africa, he pointed out that they had 'an art and a folk-lore richer and more original than that of many more advanced peoples'. – *Progress and Religion,* p.60.

If this was true of the Bushman and the Eskimo, it was evidently not less true of the sophisticated salons of eighteenth-century France, for their ideas could not be 'a mere passive result of material forces'. To Dawson the historian of ideas it was clear that the reaction against idealism and the influence of Marxism had obscured the deepest inspiration of the Revolution which at least until the summer of 1791 had to many the force of a divine revelation.

So any student of the Revolution will have to consider this passage in the fourth chapter of the present work:

'Nevertheless it could be a great mistake to ignore or to minimize the importance of the intellectual factor in the Revolution, as many modern historians have done, in reaction to the idealist conceptions of Louis Blanc and Lamartine and Michelet. If we are to deny the influence of liberalism on the French Revolution we should have to deny the influence of communism on the Revolution in Russia. In fact the movement of ideas was wider and deeper in France than in Russia and had a far greater influence on the course of events. At every stage of the Revolution, from the Assembly of the Notables in 1787 down to the fall of Robespierre in 1794, the battle of ideas decided the fate of parties and statesmen, and it was carried on not only in the National Assembly and in the meetings of the Clubs and Districts, but in the press, the streets and the cafés.'

Again it is as a historian of ideas that Dawson views the aftermath of the Revolution. No other discipline could produce his striking juxtaposition of Blake and Joseph de Maistre, so appreciative as he was of both, nor grasp the importance of Novalis's *Die Christenheit oder Europa* which, reprinted in Germany after the last war, so stimulated the movement towards European unity.

This posthumous work of Dawson's shows the breadth of mind revealed in his first books and may fix his reputation somewhat as the posthumous issue of his lectures fixed Acton's. Both were isolated scholars with a background of British independence and German scholarship. Both had a fantastic range of reading and produced less written work than their disciples demanded. Both had a high ethical fervour – Dawson spoke of 'Acton's sublime vision of a universal history which is something different from the combined history of all countries and which enlightens the mind and illuminates the soul'. That history is still unwritten, yet both were voices crying in the wilderness for its coming. Both too signed their reputations as professors in the last years of their lives, Acton at Cambridge, Dawson at Harvard.

Acton's gift for aphorism – exemplified, for instance, in his famous dictum on power, or in 'Fanaticism in religion is the alliance of the passions she condemns with the dogmas she professes' – is one shared by Dawson. One of his deepest affirms: 'Only a dying civilization neglects its dead'. Those for whom he was a chief civilizing influence in their lives will not forget that, nor him.

PART ONE

The Revolution of Ideas

I

The European Revolution

DURING the last two centuries the human race has experienced the greatest changes that it has known since the beginnings of history. Man has acquired a power over nature which surpasses the dreams of the magicians and alchemists of the past. The face of the world has been changed. New peoples have arisen in new worlds, the very existence of which was unsuspected by our medieval ancestors. The closed world of the ancient east has been thrown open and brought nearer to us than England was to Italy a century ago. Even the wild men of the jungle and the tundras have been dragged out of their prehistoric isolation and forced to conform their lives, in some manner, to western standards. Everywhere from Ireland to Japan and from Palestine to California men are wearing the same clothes, using the same machines, watching the same pictures, reading the same books and even thinking the same thoughts.

This vast transformation of human life is not due to external causes, although it may seem as universal and impersonal as the forces of nature. It is a result of the creative activity of human minds and wills: not of human mind in the abstract, but of the mind and will of concrete personalities living in a definite social environment and working in and through a definite historical tradition. For this world revolution, universal as it is in its effects, is not universal in its origins. It has its source in a particular society and a particular civilization and it has spread outward from this centre by cultural expansion and diffusion instead of by a process of independent parallel development according to the old evolutionary conception of the law of Progress.

If, then, we would understand this process of change it is not enough to study it externally, as a series of technical innovations and consequent material changes. We must study it from within as a living historical process which is material, social and spiritual. And above all we must beware of the one-sided unitary conception which interprets the whole development in terms of a single factor.

The European revolution is at once a political revolution, an economic revolution and a scientific revolution, but none of the three was the cause of the rest. They are all parallel experiences of the organic process of change which has transformed western society and the western mind during the modern age.

In the first place we must make clear what is the social organism which is the source and origin of this movement of change. For it may be objected that when we speak of western civilization or the European tradition we are making use of generalizations which are just as unreal as the abstract ideas of Civilization and Progress that have been the basis of liberal social philosophy.

In order to understand European history we must first understand what Europe is – not a mere geographical expression, nor a heterogeneous collection of independent nationalities, but a true society of peoples possessing a common tradition of culture and of religion. In the past this social organism was known as Christendom, and it is in fact in medieval Christendom that its unity is most plainly visible.

It is true that in its origins western Christendom was conterminous neither with Christendom as a whole nor with Europe. To an oriental observer it must have appeared little more than an outlying barbaric province of the Christian world, isolated between the pagan north and the Moslem south and unworthy to be compared with the wealthy and civilized society of Byzantine Christendom. Yet this semi-barbarous society of western Christendom possessed a vitality and power of growth that its more civilized neighbours lacked.

From its original centre in the Frankish dominions it

gradually extended its range, until by the end of the Middle Ages it had embraced the whole of western and northern Europe and had begun its career of colonial expansion beyond the seas, while the fortunes of eastern Christendom had steadily declined until Byzantium had become the capital of Islam and the Christian peoples of the Balkans were the slaves of the Turk.

This triumphant expansion was, however, accompanied by a loss of internal unity; western Christendom was a synthesis of Nordic and Latin elements, ordered and directed by the Church and the Papacy. The state, as it was under the tutelage of the Church and the clergy, who possessed a monopoly of the higher education, took a leading part in its administration and policy. But with the decline of feudalism and the growth of a centralized monarchical power, the state asserted its independence and attempted to deprive the territorial Church of its international character and to weaken the bonds that attached it to the Holy See.

At the same time the development of national feeling and vernacular culture brought to the surface the underlying elements of racial and cultural diversity which had been held in abeyance but not removed by the unifying forces of medieval Catholicism. Both the Latin south and the Germanic north rejected the medieval synthesis as an impure mixture of discordant elements and attempted to go behind the Middle Ages and to recover the unalloyed traditions of classical culture and evangelical religion.

Thus the sixteenth century saw the first great European revolution, a revolt carried out by the Italian Renaissance in the name of the purity of culture, and by the German Reformation in the name of the purity of the Gospel. The Middle Ages were rejected by the humanists as barbarous and by the reformers as superstitious and corrupt. To both alike they were the Dark Ages, and to both it seemed as though mankind, after a thousand years of barbarism and error, was being born again and that religion and culture were destined to be renewed after the model of primitive Christianity and classical antiquity.

But in spite of this parallelism between the two movements, they were so alien in spirit from one another that they often acted as enemies rather than allies, and their effects on European culture were entirely different. The Renaissance gradually extended its influence throughout Europe, transforming western art, literature and science and creating a common standard of education and culture that transcended political and national frontiers and thus maintained the tradition of European unity in a new form.

The Reformation, on the other hand, was a source of strife and dissension that divided Europe between hostile religious camps and warring sects. For though the Protestant Reformation did stimulate the movement of reform in southern Europe, it stimulated it by reaction, so that the movement of Catholic reform was a Counter Reformation which declared open war against the northern Reformation.

The inchoate growth of Mediterranean Protestantism was crushed between the revival of Catholicism and the hostility of northern Protestantism, and those Italian and Spanish reformers who escaped the hands of the Inquisition fell victims to the ferocious rigidity of evangelical orthodoxy, like Servetus at Geneva and Gentili at Berne.

The typical southern reformers were not Ochino and Socinus, but Ignatius Loyola and Charles Borromeo. They were in almost every respect the antithesis of the northern reformers, for they accentuated just those elements in the Christian tradition which the Protestants rejected: the principles of hierarchic authority, sacramentalism, asceticism and mysticism. And whereas the northern reformers destroyed the monasteries and abandoned the ideal of the contemplative life, the Counter Reformation found its centre of action in the new religious orders.

The alliance of this movement for Catholic reform with the Papacy and the Austro-Spanish monarchy turned the tide of Protestant revolt and reconquered much of the ground that had been lost in central and southern Europe. For a time it seemed as if the Habsburg powers would make the Holy Roman Empire a reality and restore the lost medieval unity as a centralized theocracy based on the military power of Spain and the gold of the Indies and the missionary zeal of the Jesuits. And though the realization of this dream of universal Catholic empire was frustrated by the stubborn resistance of the Huguenots and the English and the Dutch, the double monarchy of the Spanish and Austrian Habsburgs remained the most imposing political power of seventeenth-century Europe.

Thus the influence of the Counter Reformation was not confined to religion and politics; it combined with the literary and artistic traditions of the Renaissance to produce a strongly marked type of culture which transcended the limits of the Mediterranean and extended its influence over the whole Catholic world. This spirit inspired Baroque art, with its striving after infinity and intensity of emotion which renders it more akin to the art of the Middle Ages than to the rational idealism of the classical Renaissance. It was as though the Gothic spirit was expressing itself anew in classical forms.

There was no similar movement in Protestant Europe. Lutheran Germany was overshadowed by the Baroque culture of the south, while in Holland and England the whole spirit of Calvinism and Puritanism was unfavourable to the development of a religious art. It was as ferociously iconoclastic as the early Moslems; it was not only that the Puritans condemned the aesthetic hedonism of Renaissance culture as pagan and worldly, it was that their religion left no place for aesthetic expression even in the spiritual sphere. For them, even divine grace had lost its graciousness and become the irresistible engine of an inscrutable power. Human nature was so corrupted that man had become, as it were, God's natural enemy; his only hope was to be found in the bare fiat of divine will which miraculously transformed him from a child of wrath into a vessel of election predestined to fulfil the divine commands, almost in spite of himself and by no virtue or merit of his own.

But the pessimism and fatalism of Calvinist doctrine

did not lead, as we might have expected, to any loss of the sense of personal responsibility, to the depreciation of practical activity or to an ascetic flight from the world. On the contrary, Calvinism was a school of moral discipline and effort which produced self-reliant men of action, who faced a hostile world with a grim determination to do their duty and to obey the dictates of conscience at whatever cost to themselves and others.

Such a spirit was the very antithesis of Humanism. Wherever the latter asserted itself in northern Europe, as at the English court or in Dutch patrician society, it came into sharp conflict with Calvinist orthodoxy, as we see in Holland in the case of Grotius and Vondel, and in England where the highest achievement of the northern Renaissance – the Shakespearean drama – seems completely alien from the contemporary religious development of English Puritanism, as though it belonged to a different world. Consequently there was no room for the development of a synthesis between Protestantism and the Renaissance tradition such as the Catholic tradition achieved in the Baroque culture.

We have only to compare Bernini with the brothers Adam, or Saint Teresa with Hannah More, to feel the difference in the spirit and rhythm of the two cultures. The bourgeois culture has the mechanical rhythm of a clock, the Baroque the musical rhythm of a fugue or a sonata.

The conflict between these two ideals of life and forms of culture runs through the whole history of Europe from the Reformation to the French Revolution and finds its political reflection in the struggle between Spain and the Protestant powers. It is hardly too much to say that if Philip II had been victorious over the Dutch and the English and the Huguenots, modern bourgeois civilization would never have developed, and capitalism, in so far as it had existed, would have acquired an entirely different complexion.

The same spirit would have ruled at Amsterdam as at Antwerp, at Berlin as at Munich, in North America as in South; and thus the moment when Alexander Farnese turned back, a dying man, from his march on Paris may be regarded as one of the decisive points in European history, for though the Baroque culture was rigid and unprogressive, especially from the economic point of view, it was also extraordinarily stable and almost immune from internal revolutionary change. Where it had once set its foot, it remained; and it has left its imprint on regions like Flanders and Bohemia, which were geographically far removed from its original centre, and which had much closer natural and spiritual affinities to the Protestant world.

Had it not been for the existence of a kind of intermediate zone – Lutheran, Anglican, Gallican and Jansenist – between the two poles of Counter Reformation Rome and Calvinist Geneva, it is quite conceivable that Europe might have been divided between two entirely distinct and independent cultures which would have been as alien from one another as the Islamic world was from medieval Christendom.

In the seventeenth century, however, the new Protestant bourgeois culture was only beginning to assert its social and political independence, and in Europe as a whole the old social structure of medieval Christendom survived with comparatively little change. In spite of the expansion of overseas trade, and the growth of the trading cities, European society was predominantly agrarian and was still organized according to the traditional social hierarchy of nobles, clergy and peasants.

It is true that the Reformation and the dissolution of the monasteries had rendered the clergy dependent on the government and on the lay nobility throught Protestant Europe, but the whole spirit of the Lutheran tradition was intensely conservative and the caste-like rigidity of the class system rendered the social effects of the dissolution of the monasteries mainly negative.

In England also the state Church of the Tudors and the Stuarts continued to uphold the medieval ideal of an organic functional social order and the control of economic relations by an authoritarian state, while the Church gave a religious sanction to their policy by asserting that 'the most high and sacred order of kings is of Divine Right' and was entitled to the passive obedience of the subject.

The same ideas obtained in seventeenth-century France, where the Gallican Church maintained the doctrine of the Divine Right of Kings as strongly as the Anglican. Indeed Bossuet in his treatise on politics drawn from Scripture invests the royal power with quasi-divine character. The king is the image of God on earth and participates in the sovereignty and independence of the Divine power.

> The power of God [he writes] makes itself felt instantaneously from one end of the world to the other, the royal power acts at the same time throughout the kingdom. It holds the whole kingdom in being, as God holds the world. Should God withdraw His hand, the world would fall back into nothingness and should authority cease in the kingdom, all would be confusion. . . .
>
> To sum up the great and august things we have said concerning the royal authority. Behold an immense people united in a single person; behold this sacred power, paternal, absolute; behold the secret cause which governs the whole body of the state contained in a single head; you see in the king the image of God, and you have an idea of the royal Majesty. (*Politique tirée des propres paroles de L'Ecriture Sainte,* Book V, Art. IV, Prop. I).

Such conceptions have more in common with the ancient oriental and Byzantine ideal of a sacred monarchy than with modern political ideas, and they show how deeply anchored European society still was in traditions of the past.

This social traditionalism prevented the revolutionary implications of both the Reformation and the Renaissance from being widely realized; it hardly entered into men's minds that the existing order could be radically transformed. The European social order was an organic development – the result of centuries upon centuries of unconscious growth. The family and the state, kingship and authority, the different orders and classes with their functions and privileges, were not artificial creations. They had always been there and had gradually changed their form under the influence of new circumstances and different environments. And thus they were regarded as part of the natural order, ordained by God, and were accepted as men accepted the changes of the seasons and the other laws of nature.

So, too, neither religious scepticism, which had already made its appearance in the sixteenth century, nor the new science of nature, which had made such progress in the seventeenth, were yet strong enough to affect the religious background of social life. It is a mistake to suppose that European culture was secularized in the sixteenth century as a result of the Renaissance or the Reformation. Alike in Catholic and Protestant countries the seventeenth century was an intensely religious age. An occasional sceptic like Vanini or a materialist like Hobbes weighs light against the solid mass of preachers and theologians who formed public opinion and were almost the sole channels of popular instruction.

By the second half of the seventeenth century Europe seemed to have recovered from the disturbances that followed the Reformation and the age of religious war, and to have returned once more to stability and order. The close of the Thirty Years' War left the exhausted lands of central Europe craving only for peace, and utterly submitting to the will of their princes. In England, the Great Rebellion had ended in the restoration of the monarchy and the triumph of the royalist sentiment, while in Scandinavia the royal power had rendered itself absolute, both in Denmark and Sweden. But it was in the France of Louis XIV that the triumph of authority and order was most complete.

By 1650 the forces of disorder in France had been vanquished and all the material and spiritual resources of the nation were united in the vast and imposing structure of the absolute monarchical state. The absolutism of Louis XIV was at once more completely centralized and more efficiently organized than that of Philip II or the empire of

Austria. The success of French arms and diplomacy, the splendour of the court of Versailles, the national organization of economic life, the brilliant development of French literature and art under the royal patronage, all contributed to raise national prestige and to establish the political and intellectual hegemony of France in Europe.

The leadership of Catholic Europe had passed from Spain to France and from the Habsburgs to the Bourbons, and as the Baroque culture of the empire had dominated Europe in the early part of the seventeenth century, so French culture formed the standards of European taste and public opinion during the *Grand Siècle*.

The two cultures were so closely akin that the French culture of the age of Louis XIV may be regarded as a specialized form of the national form of the Baroque. But it was also a rationalization of the Baroque culture which subjected the unskilled vitality of the Baroque spirit to the rules and formulas of classical order, in the same way that in the religious sphere it subordinated the spiritual passion of Counter Reformation mysticism to the moral discipline of the patristic tradition.

But while the French classical culture possessed a logical cohesion and order which the Baroque culture itself lacked, it was a more conscious and artificial order which tended to produce a feeling of tension and constraint. Even the splendour of court life became wearisome when a noble could not absent himself from Versailles without incurring the royal displeasure. Even the grandeur of the classical style became oppressive when it left no freedom of expression for individual tastes and feelings. There were many who sought to withdraw from the ever-watchful eye of authority and to seek a freer atmosphere in which they could find relaxation and liberty to express their opinions.

This free atmosphere was not to be found in the schools and universities, which were still fortresses of authority and tradition, or in the new academies, which represented the official regimentation of intellectual life, but in the houses of nobles like the Prince of Vendôme and the salons of great ladies like Mme de Sablière and Mme de

Lambret in Paris or the Duchess of Mazarin in London, where courtiers and men of letters could meet on equal terms.

In such an atmosphere there was no room for the acrimonies of religious controversy, and intolerance became regarded as a mark of ill-breeding. Clarity of thought and wit were more highly esteemed than profundity or conviction, and the pleasures and arts of life banished the thought of death and eternity with which Puritan and Jansenist had been so painfully preoccupied. Throughout the seventeenth century there existed an undercurrent of epicurean and 'libertine' thought which links the age of Montaigne and Giordano Bruno to that of Bayle and Voltaire; and the greatest religious genius of the century, Pascal, was already acutely conscious that it was this easy-going, light-hearted scepticism, and not Protestantism or metaphysical error, which was the great danger that Catholicism had to face.

The mind of Pascal was incomparably more powerful and more profound than that of the sceptic. He had on his side all the resources of piety and scholarship and tradition. Yet he was the champion of a losing cause, while the little band of amateur philosophers, who had few convictions and were more concerned with the pleasures of life than with preaching their opinions, were the forerunners of the great movement of secular enlightenment that revolutionized European thought and changed the whole spirit of western culture.

2

The Historic Origins of
Liberalism

T H E history of the secularization of modern culture has yet to be written, and the reasons for this are easy enough to understand. For on the one hand the mind of the secularized majority has been so deeply affected by the process of secularization that it cannot view that process in an objective historical manner, while on the other the religious minority has been forced into an attitude of negative opposition which is no less unfavourable to dispassionate study. Nevertheless, it is emphatically a problem which requires an historical approach. The process of secularization was a historical movement no less than was the Reformation, a minority movement which was gradually transmitted to wider circles until it eventually won the key positions of social and intellectual influence through which it dominated European society. This movement, which was already known as the Enlightenment in the eighteenth century, and the accompanying ideology, which later acquired the name of liberalism, have long been studied by historians, chiefly in Germany and France, though in a somewhat piecemeal fashion; but their work has not hitherto been fully assimilated by educated opinion in England and America. Here the tendency has been to concentrate attention on political and economic change, and above all on the American and French revolutions. But we have not paid enough attention to the intellectual revolution that had already taken place before there was any question of a political one. Yet it is this intellectual revolution that is responsible for the secularization of

* *

western culture. This intellectual movement, like most of the movements that have changed the world, was religious in origin, although it was anti-religious in its results. It owed its dynamism to the resistance of a religious minority and its diffusion to the ill-judged and unjust, though sincere, action of religious orthodoxy. It is indeed the supreme example in history of the way in which religious persecution and repression defeats its own object and serves the cause it is attempting to destroy.

During the ten years of European peace which extended from 1678 to 1688 the power and prestige of the French monarchy reached its climax and the Catholic cause was everywhere in the ascendant. French Protestantism seemed to have received its death blow from the Revocation of the Edict of Nantes. The Protestant powers of Germany and Scandinavia were the allies and pensioners of Louis XIV. The empire had recovered from the exhaustion of the Thirty Years' War and had begun the reconquest of south-eastern Europe from the Turks and the repression of Protestantism in Hungary, which Leopold I had vowed to make 'the Kingdom of Mary'. Even the Netherlands, the great stronghold of bourgeois civilization and Calvinism, had come out of the war with France weakened, disunited and impoverished.

Nevertheless, the powers of authority and tradition were far weaker than they seemed, and the moment of their apparent triumph really marked the turn of the tide and the rallying of the forces of opposition. The attempt of Louis XIV to exterminate French Protestantism by the Revocation of the Edict of Nantes, and that of James II to secure toleration for Catholicism in England, rekindled the flames of religious warfare and aroused a passionate spirit of resistance to the supremacy of Louis XIV. The Huguenot exiles, who largely consisted of the ablest and most enterprising elements of the French bourgeoisie, were the intellectual leaders of this movement. Wherever they settled, in Holland and England and northern Germany, they formed centres of militant anti-Catholic opinion and carried on an organized campaign of public propaganda and secret agitation against the government of Louis XIV and the Catholic Church.

In this way the Huguenot diaspora acted as an intellectual ferment in western Europe and instilled a common purpose into the scattered forces of Protestantism. Nowhere was their action stronger than in the Netherlands, which were at once the centre of the new bourgeois economy and culture and of the old Calvinist spirit of opposition to Rome and the Counter Reformation monarchy. Here too they entered into relations with the exiled leaders of the English opposition who had taken refuge in Holland from the victory of the monarchical reaction in England. Here Jurieu and Claude, Bayle and Le Clerc and Basnage met Shaftesbury and Burnet and Linborch, and it was in this international atmosphere that both the plans for the English revolution and the philosophy that was to justify it were formed.

The Revolution of 1688 was the greatest victory that Protestantism had won since the independence of the Netherlands themselves, for unlike the earlier Puritan revolution, which had been directed against a Protestant king and his bishops, it united Puritans and Episcopalians in defence of their common Protestantism. It found a leader in the foremost representative of continental Protestantism, the descendant of William of Orange, and it inaugurated the long struggle against Louis XIV which broke the strength of the French monarchy and inclined the balance of European power for the first time in favour of Protestantism.

But if the Revolution of 1688 was a victory for Protestantism, it was very different from the triumph of the Kingdom of the Saints of which Milton and the Puritan idealists had dreamed. The children of the saints had become company promoters and financiers, like Nicholas Barbon, the son of Praise God Barebones, and Sir Robert Clayton, The 'extorting Ishban' of Dryden's lines.

[1] Blest times, when Ishban, he whose occupation
So long has been to cheat, reforms the nation !
Ishban of conscience suited to his trade,

They were allied with aristocratic traitors and renegades like Sutherland and Romney, and Shrewsbury and Montagu. And behind the whole combination broods the sinister genius of Shaftesbury.

Never has the influence of class interests and selfish greed been more nakedly revealed in political action. It was the victory of oligarchy and privilege over monarchy and prerogative. For the new regime was essentially a class state in which the government was controlled by the great Whig families, while the local administration was in the hands of the squirearchy. Nevertheless, the new order was by no means exclusively an agrarian one. As the Revolution owed its success to the alliance of Churchmen and Nonconformists, so the resultant social order owed its stability to the union of landlords and business men, a union which was reinforced by intermarriage and the purchase of estates by wealthy merchants and bankers. In this way the new regime acquired a distinctively bourgeois character which gradually transformed the traditional structure of English society. Under the old monarchy the government had striven to keep the several orders of the polity within their appointed limits, to maintain the corporative system in industry, to regulate wages and prices and to protect the peasants from eviction and enclosures. Now the rights of property were absolute, wages and prices were left to find their own level, and the principle of *laissez-faire* took the place of the old ideals of state regulation and corporative organization. The eighteenth century was the golden age of the great landlords and the squires, and the man of property enjoyed a freedom and a social prestige such as he had never known in the world before. But it was an age of ruin and decay for the peasants and the yeomen and the free craftsmen: it was the age of the enclosures of the commons and the destruction of the guilds; it was an age which abandoned the traditional Christian attitude to the poor and substituted a

---

As good a saint as usurer e'er made.
Absalom and Achitophel, 11, pp. 282-5.

harsher doctrine which regarded poverty as the result of sloth or improvidence and charity as a form of self-indulgence. It made self-interest a law of nature which was providentially designed to serve the good of the whole so that the love of money was transformed from the root of all evil to the mainspring of social life.

This new view of life was not, however, merely the ideological reflection of the material interests of the bourgeois class and its state. It had behind it both the moral force of Puritan individualism and the prestige of an imposing philosophical tradition. The spiritual foundations of liberalism had been laid long before the rise of the liberal state. For the germs of intellectual revolution contained in Renaissance thought were not destroyed by the temporary triumph of authority in Church and state. In fact it was in the Baroque period rather than in that of the Renaissance that the new science and the new philosophy, which revolutionized men's ideas of the universe and of human nature itself, were born. And it is an important factor in the unity of European culture that at the moment when the religious unity of Christendom was passing away, a new community of thought which transcended national and religious frontiers arose in its place. The new physical synthesis on which modern science is based was an international achievement, to which an Italian and an Englishman, a Frenchman, a Dutchman and a German – Galileo, Newton, Descartes, Huyguens and Leibniz – each contributed his share. This cosmopolitanism is less strongly marked in philosophy, where national characteristics show themselves in the contrast between the empiricism of the English philosophers, from Bacon to Locke, and the Cartesian rationalism of France. Nevertheless, both of these movements met and exchanged ideas in Holland, the great intellectual clearing house of seventeenth-century Europe, where Descartes and Hobbes, Spinoza and Locke found a home or a temporary refuge, and whence their ideas were disseminated by Huguenot publicists and cosmopolitan adventurers like Bayle and Le Clerc, Coste and Des Maiseaux, Toland and Mandeville. Thus there grew up by the end of the seventeenth century a common tradition of liberal thought to which the partisans of a new social order could appeal in their struggle with authority.

This scientific and secular current of late Renaissance thought met with the Puritan movement for political rights and religious freedom to produce the new English culture of the period of the Revolution. It is true that the Revolution was an apparent defeat for the principle of toleration, since the King (whose attitude, inspired by Penn in this matter, was perfectly sincere, in spite of the Whig historians) stood for toleration, while the Whigs fought for the Test Act and the penal laws. But the Whig leaders did not as a rule share the religious prejudices which they used as their instruments. They were in full sympathy with the new secular culture, and they aimed at a state which should represent, not the domination of a particular religion, but the real social and economic forces of the nation. The philosopher of the Revolution, John Locke, was himself a believer in toleration, and in a purely rational religion, and his theory of the state and of the origin of political authority in a social contract for the common good is purely secular in character. His whole philosophy, with its common-sense, rationalizing spirit, its rejection of all abstract ideas, and its derivation of all knowledge solely from sensible experience, was one of the great formative influences in eighteenth-century thought, and its influence extended far beyond the limits of English culture.

Even more important, however, was the work of Newton, to whom was due the final achievement of the work of Galileo and the completion of the new physical synthesis. His triumphant application of the law of gravitation to the movement of heavenly bodies justified Galileo's belief in the power of mathematics to solve the riddles of the material universe, and proved that the same physical laws held good in every part of the universe. In place of the Aristotelian doctrine that the heavens were moved by conscious spiritual substances, which derived their eternal motion from God, the unmoved mover, there was now substituted a conception of the world as a vast machine, consisting of material bodies situated in absolute space and moved by mechanical, physical laws. The ultimate realities were no longer spiritual substances and qualities but Space, Matter and Time.

Thus, at the same time that spiritual forces were being excluded from society and from human experience by the new philosophy of Hobbes and Locke, their control of the world of nature was also being denied by the new science. God was no longer seen as the heavenly King and Father, who ruled His world by the unceasing interposition of His all-seeing Providence, nor even as the Renaissance philosopher saw Him, as the immanent spiritual principle of nature. He was the Architect of the Universe, a sublime mechanic who had constructed the cosmic machine and left it to follow its own laws.

Hence the new science was as hostile to supernaturalism and to the miraculous element in Christianity as was the new philosophy, and proved one of the chief factors in the secularization of European thought. It is true that the leaders of the movement were by no means hostile to religion. Newton and Locke were good Protestants, and even the 'atheist' Spinoza was a profoundly religious man. But the religion of the philosophers was very different from that of Christian orthodoxy. It was inspired by a spirit of rationalism and naturalism which was equally hostile to the Augustinian pessimism of Calvin and to the mystical ecstasies of Baroque Catholicism. It was the product of the new lay culture that had been developing since the Renaissance, and it inherited the humanist distrust of clerical obscurantism and its resentment of the claim of the clergy to control education and thought. How widespread this anti-clerical tendency was in the seventeenth century is shown not only by the ferocious anticlericalism of Hobbes and Bayle, but by the attitude of the defenders of orthodoxy themselves: for instance, Boileau's satire on the obscurantism of the Sorbonne, and Dryden's contemptuous dismissal of the ages of faith as:

Times o'ergrown with rust and ignorance . . .
When want of learning kept the layman low,
And none but priests were authoriz'd to know;
When what small knowledge was, in them did dwell,
And he a god who could but read or spell :[2]

The orthodoxy of the classical tradition was, in fact, only maintained by a severe moral discipline, and a strong sense of authority in the state was accompanied by a revolt against the principle of authority in religion and an assertion of the supremacy of reason and the freedom of thought. It was but a step from the 'Reasonable Christianity' of Locke (1695) to the 'Christianity not Mysterious' of Toland (1696), or from the negative scepticism of Boyle to the open incredulity of Collins and Mandeville. Already in the Augustan age religion in England was exposed to a campaign of anticlerical and anti-Christian propaganda which was satirized in Swift's brilliant 'Argument against Abolishing Christianity'.[3]

Nevertheless, the immediate dangers of this movement were less serious than they appeared to contemporary believers of the type of Charles Leslie and William Law. The excesses of Deism and infidelity alarmed the man of solid Protestant bourgeois opinion, which was the real force behind the English revolution, and produced the religious reaction which characterized the middle decades of the eighteenth century. The new society found its intellectual leaders not in cosmopolitan freethinkers of the type of Toland and Bolingbroke, but in men of moderate views, like Steele and Addison and Pope, who adapted the ideals of humanist thought to the needs of the English middle classes and thus gave the Protestant bourgeois culture a classical form which was completely lacking in the undiluted Puritan tradition, as we see it in New England at this period.

[2] *Religio Laici*, pp. 370-5.
[3] 'An Argument to prove the Abolishing of Christianity in England may as things now stand be attended with some inconveniences, and perhaps not produce those many good effects proposed thereby' (1708).

In eighteenth-century England Humanism came to terms with Puritan ethics, and rationalism with Protestant theology, as represented by Samuel Clarke, Hoadly and Warburton. For the chief threat to the established order came from the Right rather than the Left, and the fear of a Jacobite counter-revolution caused the supporters of the principles of the revolution to adopt a conservative attitude in defence of the *status quo*.

Hence it was in France rather than in England that the revolutionary consequences of the new ideas were most fully realized, and the attack on the traditional Christian order was pressed farthest, though the French enlightenment owed much of its success to the achievements of the English revolution and to the influence of English ideas. But in France there was no room for a Whig compromise. The majestic unity of French absolutism and Catholicism stood like a fortress which must be destroyed before the city could be taken by the forces of liberalism and revolution. The enforcement of religious unity after the Revocation of the Edict of Nantes left no room for freedom of opinion, and the energies which found an outlet in England in the communal life of the Nonconformist sects and their theological controversies were in France driven below the surface and could only express themselves in negative criticism or in utopian idealism. Thus it is no accident that the age which saw the end of French Protestantism was followed by the age of the philosophic enlightenment; indeed the latter may be regarded as a second Reformation that carried the revolt against authority and tradition from the sphere of theology to that of secular culture. The Catholic Church still bore the brunt of the attack; indeed the new reformers repeated with monotonous insistence the abuse of priestcraft and superstition, of monkery and asceticism, of papal tyranny and scholastic obscurantism which had been the current coin of Protestant controversy for two centuries. But the state and the social order was no longer immune. Every institution and every accepted belief was submitted to the test of criticism and was summarily dismissed if deemed unreasonable or devoid of social utility. In the eyes of the new philosophers the traditional social and religious order of western Christendom was an antiquated Gothic structure which was no longer habitable. The time had come to demolish it and to construct on the *tabula rasa* of human nature a new edifice based on simple rational principles which would be suited to the needs of an enlightened society.

But the revolutionary implications of this reformation of society were only gradually realized. The earlier leaders of the Enlightenment, like Voltaire and Montesquieu, had no intention of promoting a social revolution. If they hated medievalism and clericalism, they had a profound admiration for the age of Louis XIV, and their ideal was that of a secularized and humanized classicism. When the Huguenot La Beaunelle attacked the regime of Louis XIV as an intolerant and oppressive despotism, Voltaire himself arose in defence of the King and the achievements of his reign, which he declared to be the greatest age that France or any other European nation had known. Although the French Enlightenment was closely related to the rise of the bourgeoisie and the development of a new bourgeois mentality, the French bourgeoisie was a very different class from that which created the new capitalist society in Holland and England and America. In France the state had kept a tight hand on trade and industry, and the policy of Louis XIV and Colbert left no room for the development of an independent financial power like that of the financiers who ruled the Dutch and English East India Companies, and the Bank of Amsterdam and the Bank of England. The typical French financier was a servant of the government, a treasurer or tax farmer; and even the bankers, like Samuel Bernard, the great Huguenot capitalist under Louis XIV, were more concerned with the negotiation of public loans than with ordinary commercial or industrial credit.

Consequently the French bourgeoisie looked to the state rather than to private enterprise for employment and social advancement. It was the ambition of the rich mer-

chant or lawyer to purchase some office which would open
a career for his son in the public service. To a greater extent
than any other European country France was a state of
lawyers and officials. The French bureaucracy, 'the order
of officers' as it was called, formed a kind of bourgeois
aristocracy, distinct in character and origin from the feudal
nobility; even the great ministers of Louis XIV, such as
Colbert, were often men of humble origin. It is true that in
the eighteenth century the path of advancement grew more
difficult, and that the *noblesse de robe* became more and
more a closed caste. Nevertheless, wide as was the gulf
between great magistrates like Montesquieu and Henault,
and lawyers like Mathieu Marais or the father of Voltaire,
they possessed a unity of traditions, interests and ideas
similar to that which unites the commissioned and noncom-
missioned officers in an army, or the prelates and the clergy
in the church.

The predominance of this legal and official class is
reflected in the development of French society and culture
during the seventeenth and eighteenth centuries. It showed
itself in the sense of logic and order, the insistence on
abstract principles and rights, and the jealousy of clerical
domination which inspired educated lay opinion. It was
this class which created the classical culture and the abso-
lutist state of the *Grand Siècle* by the administrative genius
of the archbureaucrat Colbert and the intellectual leadership of men like Racine and Boileau, Pascal and Descartes,
Bossuet and Malebranche, all members of the *noblesse de
robe*, the bourgeois official class.[4] In the eighteenth century
this class remained as important as ever, but it was no
longer controlled by the firm hand of a great king like
Louis XIV, whose strict religious principles and intense
devotion to duty made him the embodiment of the bureaucratic ideal of monarchy. The court of the regent, on the

[4] The chief exceptions are Fénelon, St Simon and St Evremond,
who were aristocrats, and Molière and Bayle who were bourgeois,
and these were just the writers who were the least sympathetic to the
regime of Louis XIV.

other hand, outraged all the traditions of the bourgeoisie by its immorality and luxury, while the abortive attempt of the new government to restore the political role of the nobility antagonized the Parlement of Paris and the bureaucracy. The official class became animated by a spirit of opposition and disaffection which was a constant source of embarrassment to the French government throughout the eighteenth century. It was not atheists or demagogues who undermined the stately order of the *Grand Siècle*. Long before the Revolution the authority of the crown was challenged by the official representatives of legality, and the orthodoxy of the Church was discredited by the partisans of theological traditionalism. The two movements of political and religious opposition were closely related, and nowhere are the characteristics of the official parliamentary caste more clearly defined than in the leaders of the Jansenist movement like the great Arnauld and Nicole and M. de Sacy. But it was not until the eighteenth century that Jansenism became almost identified with the parliamentary opposition and degenerated into a narrow and bitter sect which did more to discredit the cause of religion than all the attacks of the philosophers. It was Jansenism which first created the bourgeois anticlericalism that appears so clearly in the journals of men like Mathieu Marais. And it was this spirit of Jansenist anticlericalism which prepared the way for the downfall of the Jesuits and thus shook the very foundations of the Baroque culture.

But though the Jansenist opposition divided and weakened the forces of tradition, it was powerless to create a new order. It was itself a lost cause – a kind of religious Jacobitism – which was condemned to struggle in vain against the rising tide of Enlightenment. It was not in the dusty atmosphere of the Sorbonne and the Parlements that the spirit of the new age found expression, but in the great world of the court and the salons, where the cult of pleasure and the pursuit of social success were too seductive for men to trouble themselves with the austere demands of Jansenist morality. As we have seen, the tradition of free thinking and loose living was already well established in

French aristocratic society during the seventeenth century. But it was in the eighteenth century, during the reign of Louis XV, that it passed from the nobles to the bourgeois and developed into the great movement of ideas which secularized French culture. Voltaire, the foremost representative of this movement, was himself a member of the lawyer class, who preferred the career of letters to the career for which his father had destined him and who by sheer literary talent attained a position of greater wealth and social importance than any commoner in Europe had hitherto achieved. In this he served the interests of his class no less than his own, for he did more than anyone else to raise the profession of letters from the proletarian squalor of Grub Street and its servile dependence on noble patrons to an independent power in European society – a fourth estate which could meet princes and ministers on an equal footing and influence the fortunes of nations. Voltaire graduated in the liberation society of the Regency – at the Temple and the salons of the Duchess of Maine – and his mind never lost the imprint of the Regency tradition. But his bourgeois spirit revolted against the arbitrary pride and inequality of aristocratic society and it was in the England of the Whig Revolution rather than in the France of the Regency that he found his philosophic vocation.

Here it is true, he was following in the footsteps of many another French exile, like the Huguenots Leclerc, Coste and Desmaiseaux, but he was by far the greatest of the apostles of English ideas, and his visit to England in 1726, which was followed by Montesquieu's in the next year, marks an epoch in the history of French thought.

Voltaire and Montesquieu found in England a society that was the direct antithesis of all that they had known in France – one in which the crown had no control over the legislature or the administration of justice, and in which the greatest freedom of thought and expression prevailed, alike in political and religious matters. They were impressed by the vigorous individualism of English life, and by the economic and social prosperity by which it was accompanied, but most of all by its frankly secular and anticlerical spirit. For they had discovered England in the age of the Deists and the Freethinkers, before the great Wesleyan religious revival, the imminence of which they could hardly suspect. 'Point de religion en Angleterre', says Montesquieu – and this was the feature of English life which most appealed to the mind of Voltaire. He ascribed it to the victory of the new philosophy of Newton and Locke, and accordingly he made this the basis of his own philosophic propaganda in France. His first influential work, *The Philosophic or English Letters,* which begins with a discussion of the English sects and praise of English toleration, finds its centre in an exposition of the ideas of Newton and Locke, whom he hails as the greatest minds of the human race. 'From Plato to Locke, there is nothing', he says; and later D'Alembert summed up the judgement of his age when he declared Locke to be the creator of metaphysics as Newton had been the creator of physics.

The philosophic propaganda achieved an extraordinary success in France. The new ideas were taken up by the fashionable world, and were debated in the salons of great ladies and fashionable financiers. With the publication of the great *Encyclopaedia,* from 1751 onwards they received as it were an official statement, and became the creed of an organized party, which gained adherents wherever the influence of French culture was dominant, from Berlin to Naples.

But the movement had undergone a profound change in passing from England to the continent. As we have seen, the Whig Revolution was based on the sturdy individualism of Protestant bourgeois society, and the new English culture represented a compromise between the Puritan and the humanist tradition. In France, on the other hand, the new ideas were introduced into a society which had been drilled into uniformity by the combined influences of the Counter Reformation Church and the Baroque monarchy, and which possessed a complete unity of culture and religion. The philosophers found themselves opposed, not to a fluctuating mass of warring sects, but to a single Church which claimed absolute authority over thought and morals. Hence the openly anti-Christian character of the philosophic movement, of which the watchword was Voltaire's 'Ecrasez l'infame', and which ultimately led to the celebration of the Feast of Reason in the Cathedral of Notre Dame. Though they might invoke the principle of toleration, as practised in England, their real aim was to replace one unity by another, to substitute the universal reign of science and reason for that of religion and authority. This absolutism of thought, so utterly unlike the cautious realism of the English thinkers, was due not only to the violence of the intellectual struggle, but to the whole tendency of the French mind. The men of the age had an unlimited belief in the powers of human reason and in the possibility of an immediate social transformation if only the legislature could be won over to the cause of reason and progress. But they had no desire for political or social revolution and little sympathy with democratic ideals. Almost to a man the philosophers, like their predecessors the English Whigs, were on the side of property and order. Their ideal was an authoritarian liberalism based on the union of the government and the intelligentsia,[5] and they were never so happy as when they were acting as the confidential advisers of kings and ministers, as Voltaire did with Frederick II, and Choiseul and Diderot with Catherine the Great.

In spite of the vein of Utopian socialism which comes to the surface in writers like Morelly, the author of the *Code de la nature*, and the Abbé Mably, the philosophers would have been horrified at the idea of transferring power from rulers like Frederick the Great and Catherine of Russia, or from ministers like Choiseul and Turgot, to the common people. Voltaire in particular had an unbounded contempt for the populace the '*canaille* that is not worthy of enlightenment and which deserves its yoke'. He was himself a capitalist who had accumulated an enormous

[5] It is a pity that the eighteenth century did not know this useful neologism, for the class to which it refers has never been more defined, more conscious and more influential than in France during this period.

fortune by loans and speculation and careful investment, and no one could have had a stronger sense of property or a greater desire to make the most of the social position he had achieved. He was a true liberal, but his liberalism had in it nothing visionary or utopian. In fact, as M. Lanson remarks, the Voltairean ideal found its realization in the bourgeois France of Louis Philippe.[6] Even in intellectual matters the philosophers were by no means in favour of universal enlightenment. 'I doubt', writes Voltaire, 'if the populace has either the time or the capacity for education. They would die of hunger before they became philosophers. It seems to be essential that there should be ignorant beggars. If you had to improve a property or if you had ploughs, you would agree with me. It is not the worker we must instruct, it is the bon bourgeois of the townsman.'[7] 'We have never pretended to enlighten shoemakers and servant girls, that is the portion of the apostles.'[8]

In fact, as David Mornet points out, it was the Church that worked almost alone, but not unsuccessfully, for the cause of popular education, while the philosophers were content to devote their energies to the enlightenment of the 'little flock' of rich, well-born well-educated people who make public opinion. Here their propaganda proved extraordinarily successful. With the fall of the Jesuits the Church lost its influence over the mind of the ruling classes and the philosophers took the place of the confessor as the spiritual guide of kings and ministers. The movement reached its height during the generation before the French Revolution, the age of Joseph II in Austria and his brother Leopold in Tuscany, Catherine II in Russia, Gustav III in Sweden, Struensee in Denmark, Florida Blanca in Spain, and Turgot and Malesherbes in France. Even before this time the new ideas were at work in France under Choiseul and Mme de Pompadour, in Prussia under Frederick the Great, in Austria under Kaunitz, in Naples under Tanucci, and in Portugal under Pombal. Throughout Europe states-

[6] G. Lanson, *Voltaire*, p. 80.
[7] To Damilaville, 1 April 1766.
[8] *Ibid.*, 6 December 1757.

men were engaged in sweeping away the debris of the
Middle Ages and carrying out administrative, social and
economic reforms according to the principles of the new
philosophy. But though the success of this movement was
rapid and widespread, it was also limited and superficial.
Underneath the surface of rational enlightenment the life
of the peasants and the craftsmen followed the old ways of
social and religious traditions. While the courtiers of
Catherine II or Joseph II read the latest books from Paris
and adopted the fashionable rationalism of cosmopolitan
society, their peasant serfs still lived in the world of
Baroque Catholicism or Byzantine orthodoxy. And hence
there developed a spiritual cleavage in society which contained the seeds of class conflict and social revolution. In the
old Christian order nobles and peasants had shared a
common faith and a common service. But now that
Christianity was regarded as only good for the lower
classes, as Voltaire so often asserts, the spiritual foundation
of social unity was destroyed. In spite of all that the
enlightened despots and their ministers did for the cause of
civilization and progress they had lost the sacred character
of the old Christian kingship, which had invested even the
unimpressive exterior of the later Habsburgs with the aura
of divinity. And with the loss of this tradition the heart
went out of the *ancien régime* and left it a hollow shell. It
is true that in certain respects European culture has never
reached a higher level than it did in France during the Age
of the Enlightenment. Never has the art of living been
more cultivated, never has society been more open to ideas
and more ready to appreciate and reward intellectual
talent; but all the graces of life – the famous *douceur de
vivre* of which Talleyrand speaks – were often a brilliant
façade which had nothing but a spiritual void behind it.
The men who were loyal to the old tradition, like Dr
Johnson, had their hearts in the right place, however
narrow and bigoted they were in their views. But there is a
repellent   heartlessness   about   the   leaders   of   the
Enlightenment, like Frederick the Great and Voltaire and
Chesterfield and Horace Walpole and Talleyrand, which is

the peculiar weakness of a purely rational culture.[9] Hence there arose a reaction against the Enlightenment, which asserted the rights of the heart against the dictatorship of reason, and created a new religion of feeling which did more than all the reasonings of the philosophers to create a new social order. The answer to Voltaire came neither from the Sorbonne nor from the Jansenists, but from Rousseau.

[9] Consider, for example, the refusal of Kaunitz to visit his dying emperor and friend because he could not bear the sight of sick people.

3

The Birth of Democracy

T H E origins of modern democracy are so closely bound up with the history of liberalism that it is a matter of considerable difficulty to disentangle them and to distinguish their distinctive contributions to the common political-tradition of modern western culture. For this question also involves that of the relation between the three revolutions, the English, the American, and the French, which transformed the Europe of the *ancien régime*, with its absolute monarchies and state churches, into the modern world. Now all these three revolutions were liberal revolutions and all of them were political expressions of the movement of the European enlightenment in its successive phases. But this movement was not originally a democratic one and it was only in the second half of the eighteenth century that the democratic ideal was clearly formulated. On the continent of Europe the revolution of ideas preceded the political and economic revolutions by half a century, and the revolution of ideas was not in any sense of the word a democratic movement; it was the work of a small minority of men of letters who looked to the nobles and the princes of Europe rather than to the common people, and whose ideal of government was a benevolent and enlightened absolutism, like that of Frederick the Great or the Empress Catherine of Russia. There was an immense gulf between the ideas of Voltaire and Turgot, of Diderot and D'Alembert, and the opinions of the average man. The liberalism of the philosophers was a hothouse growth which could not be easily acclimatized to the open air of the fields and the market place.

No doubt the culture of the Enlightenment had an

international diffusion which added to its prestige and influence, so that if we judge from literary evidence alone we should conclude that the cause of liberalism was already won. But it was a superficial triumph which affected an infinitesimal portion of European society; outside the circle of the privileged and educated minority the vast majority of the population still followed the old ways and accepted the beliefs and ideas of their forefathers. The forces that have unified the modern world – industrialism, mechanical transport, journalism, public education and universal military service – did not exist, and society was made up of countless regional units which were economically self-contained and possessed their own traditions and customs, and often even their own laws and institutions.

This regionalism found its extreme development in the little states and ecclesiastical principalities of Germany, which was a perfect museum of medieval survivals; but even in France, which was the most unified continental state, the influence of the feudal past still made itself felt in the diversity of provincial institutions, each of which had its own economic life only remotely affected by the fashions and opinions of the great world. The Church still maintained its power over men's minds, and its festivals and pilgrimages played a great part in the life of the people. There was a deep undercurrent of religious life in the Age of Enlightenment which is none the less important for being ignored by the philosophers and men of letters. The age of Voltaire and Bolingbroke and Frederick the Great was also the age of Wesley and Tersteegen[1] and St Paul of the Cross.[2] It is true that this movement is most evident in the Protestant world, with the Moravians and Pietists in Germany, the Methodists in England, and the Great Awakening in America, but it was by no means lacking in Catholic Europe during the eighteenth century, as we see from the foundation of the new missionary orders in Italy,

[1] Protestant mystic and religious poet, 1697-1764, of Muhlheim on Ruhr.

[2] (1694-1775); founder of the Passionist Order in Italy, 1720.

the building of great baroque monasteries and pilgrimage churches such as Wies, Vierzehnheiligen, Melk, and Neresheim in Germany and Austria, and the vitality of popular religious life. Nothing shows the divorce between the bourgeois rationalism of the Enlightenment and the religious traditions of popular culture better than the figure of the beggar saint Benedict Joseph Labre (1748-83), who lived the life of a medieval ascetic and miracle worker in the age of Gibbon and Adam Smith.

But in spite of its internal resources the Church, because of its close alliance with the state, was rendered exceptionally vulnerable to any attack from above. Consequently the substitution of the enlightened despotism of Joseph II and Choiseul and Charles III of Spain for the Catholic absolutism of the Baroque period deprived the Church of its traditional method of social action, and neutralized its activities for two generations. The situation was ripe for the rise of a new spiritual force which would fill the void created by the temporary breakdown of Catholic action, and give an outlet to the religious instincts that found no satisfaction in the rational culture of the Enlightenment. For the Enlightenment had swept and garnished the western mind without bringing anything to take the place of the religion that it had destroyed. The typical man of the age, like Voltaire or Frederick the Great or Horace Walpole, was the final product of an aristocratic humanist culture. He had all the gifts that a purely intellectual culture would bestow, but the hard polished surface of his mind reflected light without warmth. If the liberal ideas of the Enlightenment were to penetrate beyond the limited world of the privileged classes and change the thought and the life of the people, they had to make an appeal to psychological forces that lay beneath the surface of rational consciousness. They had to be transformed from a philosophy into a religion: to cease to be mere ideas and to become articles of faith.

This reinterpretation of liberalism in religious terms was the work of Jean-Jacques Rousseau, who thus became the founder and prophet of a new faith – the religion of democracy. The son of a watchmaker of Geneva, *déclassé et déraciné*, he came into the world of the salons from the borders of that religious underworld which the philosophers had despised or ignored. In spite of his conversion to Catholicism he preserved the uncompromising religious individualism of Genevan Protestantism, and though he was converted from Catholicism to liberalism he retained a sentiment of attachment to the piety of the priests and religious men, like the Abbé Gaime and Père Hemet, who had befriended him in his youth. Consequently he felt himself an alien and an outsider in the society of the philosophers, and looked on the brilliant, materialistic culture of eighteenth-century Paris with the resentful and disapproving eyes of a Puritan and a man of the people. In 1749, as he walked to Vincennes on a hot autumn afternoon to visit Diderot, he experienced a sudden flash of inspiration which revealed to him his true mission and converted him from an unsuccessful man of letters into the prophet of a new gospel. He saw that all the ills of man and all the evils of society were due not to man's own sin or ignorance but to social injustice and the corruptions of an artificial civilization. If man could return to nature and follow the divinely inspired instincts of his own heart, all would be well. The savage child of nature was happier than the spoiled child of civilization, and the simple faith of the peasant wiser than all the science of the philosophers.

This creed, which finds its earliest expression in Rousseau's *Discourses on the Arts and Sciences* (1750) and in the *Origin of Inequality* (1753), was the theme of all his subsequent works. He applies it to religion in his *Letter to Voltaire on Providence* (1756) and in his *Profession of Faith of a Curate of Savoy;* to marriage and the family in *La Nouvelle Héloïse*; to education in *Émile*; and to politics in the *Social Contract*. He pleads the cause of the individual against society, the poor against the rich, and the people against the privileged classes, the cause of love against convention, and of intuition and religious sentiment against the philosophers and the libertines.

It is impossible to exaggerate the effect of Rousseau's teaching on his generation. It came into the brilliant artificial world of the Enlightenment like a warm west wind from the fields into a lighted salon, extinguishing the tapers and filling the air with the scent of damp earth and rain-soaked vegetation. No wonder that the aged Voltaire gnashed his teeth in rage at the daring of this madman and charlatan who was a traitor to the philosophic cause and who divided the forces of progress. For it was no longer to Voltaire but to Rousseau that the new generation turned for guidance and inspiration. He was the spiritual father of the makers of the new age, and the source of that spirit of revolutionary idealism which finds expression not only in liberalism but in socialism and anarchism as well. It was he who first fired men's minds with the ideal of democracy not as a mere system of government but as a new way of life, a vision of social justice and fraternity which is nothing else than the kingdom of God on earth. It is true that Rousseau himself was not a revolutionary in the ordinary sense. The revolution that he preached was not a political or an economic one but a spiritual one, and he fully realized the practical danger of any sudden disturbance of the existing order. But these cautious reservations did little to lessen the effect of his tremendous denunciation of the inequality and injustice of the existing social order. Although he was no socialist, he had no sympathy with the ideals of the capitalist economy; and though he admired the freedom and republican simplicity of Swiss Protestant society, he denounced its spirit of bourgeois individualism. 'You are merchants, mechanics, bourgeois, always occupied with private interest, business, and profits,' he wrote to the citizens of Geneva, 'you are people to whom liberty itself is only a means of acquisition without risk, and of possession with security.'[3]

This anti-bourgeois and anti-commercial tendency distinguished the liberalism of Rousseau alike from that of the Whig Revolution, which was based on the rights of Property even more than the Rights of Man, and from that

[3] Letters from the Mountain.

of the Enlightenment, which was favourable to capitalism and found its most enthusiastic supporters among the financiers and their wives.[4] Rousseau, like Mably, was profoundly hostile to the apologists of luxury, like Mandeville and Voltaire, and to the representatives of economic liberalism such as Turgot and Adam Smith. Here he was on the side not only of conservative critics of the Enlightenment like Linguet and the Marquis of Mirabeau, but still more of champions of orthodoxy like the Abbé Prigent and Père Hyacinthe Gasquet, who maintained the traditional Catholic doctrine with regard to usury and the rights of the poor. As Groethuysen has shown with copious illustrations from eighteenth-century preachers and theologians, the Church down to the eve of the Revolution maintained a stiff opposition to the capitalist philosophy and the economic view of life which were already triumphant in Protestant England and Holland. For behind the open battle of the Enlightenment which was being fought out on the ground of philosophy and freedom of thought, there was a deeper and more obscure struggle being waged by the bourgeois spirit, not only against the traditional order, which limited the freedom of commerce and bound industry within the narrow frontiers of the Corporation or Guild, but also against the religious tradition which idealized poverty and condemned the acquisitive and competitive spirit which was inseparable from the new commercial society. In this battle Rousseau was on the side of the reactionaries, and his denunciations of wealth have the same motive and inspiration as those of Bourdaloue or Croiset. His economic ideal was the agrarian distributivism of peasant society inspired by the traditional Christian ideals of charity and mutual aid and it had nothing in common with the competitive individualism of capitalist society or with the industrial mass organization of modern socialism. Nor was this ideal entirely divorced from the realities of his age, for the question of the peasant was the

[4] Helvetius was himself a financier, Mme D'Epinay was the wife of one, and Mme Dupin was the daughter of the great banker Samuel Bernard.

vital social problem of his era and the only possible form of democracy was one based on peasant ownership and peasant citizenship. The Revolution itself was to show that neither the bourgeoisie nor the urban populace was capable of realizing Rousseau's ideal of republican democracy.

Rousseau himself, however, had no wish to apply his principles to a large, highly centralized state like eighteenth-century France. He believed that political equality was unattainable unless economic conditions were favourable to social equality, and that democratic institutions were only suitable to small states whose citizens could participate directly in public life and government, such as the Swiss peasant cantons or the city states of antiquity.

But while his eyes were turned to the past, towards an idealized picture of Sparta and Rome, a democratic state was actually coming into existence in the new world across the Atlantic, and there is a curious analogy between the philosophical abstractions of Rousseau's theory of democracy and the historical realities of American democracy. A century and a half before the *Social Contract* was written, the little band of Puritan exiles who landed on the virgin shores of New England signed a real Social Compact by which they constituted themselves a 'civil body politic' and promised their individual obedience to the general will. And this was but a new development of the Calvinist principle of the Church covenant – 'a visible Covenant, Agreement, or consent whereby they give themselves unto the Lord for the observing of the ordinances of Christ together in the same society' – a principle which inspired the whole development of society in New England. It was on this basis that the town – the primary social unit – was founded, so that the Church, the school and the town meeting were all organs of one spiritual community which exercised a strict control over the moral and economic life of its members. This democratic theocracy, with its intensive moral discipline and its strong communal spirit, was the creative force behind the American development. It is true, as James Truslow Adams insists, that it was narrow, intolerant and repressive, and that it excluded a large part of the population from Church membership and civic rights. Nevertheless, the congregational ideal was essentially democratic, and the basing of citizenship on membership of the Church and Church membership on personal conversion gave the whole social system a unitary character such as it could never have gained from purely political institutions. It meant that society was not an external order imposed on the individual by authority and tradition, but a spiritual community in which membership involved a personal act of conviction and self-surrender. This contractual or 'covenanting'[5] principle of social order has an obvious analogy to Rousseau's theory, allowing for the theological difference between the strict Calvinism of the seventeenth-century New Englanders and the liberal Protestantism of the eighteenth-century citizens of Geneva. But there was another element in New England society with which he would have had less sympathy. Behind the Puritan colonization in America there was the economic enterprise of the Puritan capitalists who financed the ventures. The government of Massachusetts was in the hands of a joint stock company and it was the transference of the Charter to New England by the emigration of capitalists like John Winthrop and Isaac Johnson, the brother-in-law of the Earl of Lincoln, that secured the self-sufficiency and independence of the new colony. Nevertheless, the capitalism of the proprietors of the Massachusetts Company, as

[5] 'Having undertaken for the glory of God and advancement of the Christian Faith and honour of our King and countrie, a voyage to plant the first colony in the Northern parts of Virginia, [we] do by these present solemnly and mutually in the presence of God and one of another, covenant and combine ourselves together into a civill body politick, for our better ordering and preservation and forthcome of the ends aforesaid; by virtue hereof to enacte, constitute and frame such just and equall Lawes, ordinances, Acts, constitutions and offices, from time to time, as shall be thought most meete and convenient for the generall good of the colonie : unto which we promise all due submission and obedience, in witness wherof we have hereunder subscribed our names, at Cape Cod the eleventh of November—A.D. 1620' J. Bradford, *History of the Plymouth Plantation*, ed. C. Deane (1861), pp. 89ff.

later that of William Penn in Pennsylvania, Lord
Baltimore in Maryland, and Oglethorpe in Georgia, was
inspired by religious idealism rather than private interest.
Moreover, though the colonial society was the creation of
the same social and religious forces which produced the
new commercial bourgeois culture in Holland and
England, it developed in a very different environment from
that of the European bourgeois. Instead of the old world of
social privilege and economic competition, the American
colonist found himself back in the state of nature – not the
idealized nature of Rousseau's dreams, but the savage
reality of the forest and the war trail and the scalping
knife. The two fundamental facts which conditioned
American social development were the unlimited supplies
of unoccupied land, which made every able-bodied free
man a potential land owner, and the fear of Indians and
famine, which forced the frontier population (and in the
beginning all settlements were frontier settlements) to
sacrifice their natural individualism to the need for co-
operation and combination against the dangers that
threatened them. These conditions were common to New
England and Virginia: the only difference was the difference of social structure between the Anglican, slave-owning
democracy of the south, where the social unit was the
individual plantation,[6] and the Congregationalist farming
democracy of New England, where the social unit was the
township with its common fields and communal spirit.
These differences were accentuated in the eighteenth century, owing to the increase of Negro slavery, which
favoured the development of large, self-sufficient estates in
the south and the widening of the class division between
the aristocratic planters and the democracy of small farmers
and squatters. On the other hand, a somewhat parallel
development was taking place in New England during the

[6] The institutional unit in the south was the parish, but owing
to the scattered population on the plantations, strung out for miles
along the rivers, the southern parish never had the social importance
of the New England town.

same period, owing to the growth of capitalism, which showed itself in land speculation as well as in the rise of a wealthy merchant class.

Thus the first half of the eighteenth century saw a decline of the simplicity and equality which had marked colonial society in the previous century. The wealthy planters and merchants of the earlier seaboard were drawn into closer relations with English society and were influenced by contemporary European standards of life and thought. The churches had lost their control over political life and the closed theocratic orderly world of Puritan society disintegrated under the pressure of economic change and the growing secularization of culture. Nevertheless, the influence of the coast was counterbalanced by that of the frontier, which reproduced and even accentuated the primitive conditions of the early settlements so that every extension of the area of settlement brought a fresh addition to the democratic elements in the population. Moreover, under the surface the Puritan tradition still retained its power and vitality, as we see from the Great Awakening of 1740 and the development of sectarian activity that followed it. It was in the eighteenth century that American Puritanism produced its greatest religious teacher, Jonathan Edwards; and about the same time the diary and writings of the Quaker John Woolman (1720-72) show that the religion of the people sometimes possessed a strain of social idealism no less high and even more profound than that of the liberal Enlightenment. Woolman denounces social injustice and corruption no less strongly than Rousseau, but instead of confining himself to generalities he spent his life working against the iniquities of slavery and the acquisitive spirit that was characteristic of the new bourgeois society.

But in spite of this continued vitality of religious tradition among the people, the culture of the upper and middle classes were affected by the same movement of rational Enlightenment that was triumphant in western Europe. The greatest representative of this American

Enlightenment was the Boston printer and journalist Benjamin Franklin, who settled in Pennsylvania in 1726 and gradually built up an intercolonial and international reputation as scientist, politician and moralist. His common sense, his practical spirit, his industry and economy, his philanthropy and moral optimism, made him an example of all the bourgeois virtues, and yet he possessed at the same time a democratic simplicity and *bonhomie* which appealed to the disciples of Rousseau and the leaders of enlightened opinion in France.[7] Thus to the European world Franklin became a representative figure who embodied the new democratic ideal of a humanity, liberated from the restraints of privilege and tradition and recognizing no laws but those of nature and reason, while in America he was no less important as marking the rise of a new national culture that transcended the provincial and sectarian limitations of the earlier period.

It was inevitable that this growth of national consciousness should also find political expression. But Franklin's scheme for the creation of a colonial union under the crown in 1754 failed to overcome the spirit of separation and provincialism, and a basis of union was only to be found in the common opposition of the different colonies to the centralizing tendencies of the crown and the British Parliament. The destruction of the French empire in North America during the Seven Years' War at last freed the colonies from their dependence on British military support and made them more conscious than ever of their political and economic dependence on the mother country. Moreover, at the very moment when a revision of imperial relations had become inevitable, George III was becoming more and more involved in a political conflict with the Whigs and was returning to the traditional alliance

[7] John Adams wrote that 'if a collection could be made of all the gazettes of Europe for the latter half of the eighteenth century, a greater number of panegyrical paragraphs upon "le grand Franklin" would appear, it is believed, than upon any other man that ever lived.

between the crown and the Tories. The colonial opposition felt that it represented not only local interests but Whig constitutional principles and the traditions of the English Revolution. The political philosophy of Sidney and Locke provided a common platform on which the representatives of the American Enlightenment, like Franklin and Jefferson, could unite with the leaders of the Puritan democracy of New England, such as Samuel Adams, in the same way as the Whig aristocrats had combined with the Protestant bourgeoisie in 1688.

But whereas the social structure of English society had given a preponderance to the aristocratic landowning interests in the Whig settlement, the decisive factor in the American situation was the strength of the popular element, which gave the struggle a democratic character. In New England especially it was not the wealthy merchants nor even the enfranchised farmer who initiated the revolutionary movement; it was the unenfranchised populace, organized into secret societies like the Sons of Liberty, who dominated the town meetings and overawed the merchants and the loyalists by mob law and mass terrorism. This popular hostility to the British government was the chief cause of the success of the Revolution, and this hostility was due to social and economic causes rather than to the constitutional questions which occupied the attention of the lawyers and politicians. Westminster was a long way from Boston and the attitude of the average man to the British government was determined by his hatred of the excise man and the informer. So, too, the frontiersmen resented the closing of the western frontier to settlement, and saw the authority of the crown as a sinister power in league with the proprietors and land speculators who so often challenged their titles to the lands that they had won from the wilderness. Finally, there was the religious influence of the Puritan and Nonconformist tradition which gave the New Englander and the southern Presbyterian a sense of independence and spiritual alienation from the Anglican monarchy which had persecuted their ancestors and from which they had escaped to found a new 'Bible Commonwealth' based on the pure word of God.[8]

It is true that as the movement of revolt became politically self-conscious, the leadership was inevitably taken by the non-democratic elements, lawyers, politicians, and men of wealth and position like Washington and the Lees. But the driving force behind the movement was a democratic one, and even among the leaders there were representatives of the Enlightenment, like Franklin in Pennsylvania and Jefferson in Virginia, through whom the democratic principles implicit in the American Revolution finally received their classical formulation in the Declaration of Independence. For the progress of the controversy itself had forced the lawyers and politicians to abandon the narrow ground of constitutional precedent and to fall back on the fundamental dogmas of the new religion. 'The sacred rights of mankind', wrote Hamilton, 'are not to be rummaged for among old parchments or musty records. They are written, as with a sunbeam, in the whole volume of human nature by the hand of Divinity itself, and can never be erased or obscured.'

But it was not in the writings of Hamilton or Jefferson that this appeal to the ultimate principles of democracy found its clearest expression. It was Thomas Paine, an obscure English excise man, but recently landed in America with Franklin's letter of introduction, who finally brought the confused democratic aspirations of the American people to a full awareness of their revolutionary aims. In *Common Sense,* his famous pamphlet, he swept the legal and constitutional issues impatiently aside and appealed in flaming rhetoric for the liberation of humanity and the creation of a new world:

O ye that love mankind [he writes], ye that dare oppose not only tyranny but the tyrant, stand forth; every spot of the old

---

[8] The importance of this religious motive is shown by the fact that Anglicanism throughout the northern colonies was almost solidly loyalist, while even in Virginia an attack on the position of the established church, led by the Presbyterian Patrick Henry, preceded the constitutional struggle.

world is overcome with oppression. Freedom has been hunted round the globe. Asia, Africa have long expelled her. Europe regards her like a stranger, and England hath given her warning to depart! O! receive the fugitive and prepare in time an easy home for mankind.

We have it in our power to begin the world over again. A situation similar to the present hath not happened since the days of Noah until now. The birthday of a new world is at hand, and a race of men perhaps as numerous as all Europe contains are to receive their portion of freedom from the event of a few months. The reflection is awful – and in this point, how trifling, how ridiculous do the little paltry cavillings of a few weak or interested men appear, when weighed against the business of a world.[9]

In this pamphlet we meet, I believe for the first time, two features which were to become characteristic of the revolutionary movement of the future. One was the conception of political revolution as part of a universal and almost cosmic change which far transcended the local and historical circumstances of any particular state.[10] The other, which is closely related, was the note of messianic idealism, which looked forward to a social millennium and the birth of a new humanity. Neither of these elements had been of any importance in the previous history of the English Revolution of 1688 or the French Enlightenment. They have their roots in the revolutionary and apocalyptic tendencies of the Protestant Reformation among the Anabaptists and the millenniarist sects, and it is the union of these elements with the rationalism and naturalism of the Enlightenment, which was first achieved by Thomas

[9] *Common Sense* (2nd ed., 1776), pp. 58 and 59.
[10] 'What we formerly called Revolutions', wrote Paine fifteen years later, 'were little more than a change of persons, or an alteration of local circumstances. They rose and fell like things of course, and had nothing in their existence or their fate that could influence beyond the spot that produced them. But what we now see in the world, from the Revolutions of America and France, are a renovation of the natural order of things, a system of principles as universal as truth and the existence of man, and combining moral with political happiness and national prosperity.'

Paine, that marks the definite emergence of the modern revolutionary creed. Owing to the influence of Paine, Jefferson and Franklin, the American cause became identified in the eyes of the world with this revolutionary idealism, and the conflict was transformed from a local quarrel concerning taxation and colonial rights into a crusade for the rights of man and the cause of humanity.

Nowhere did it find more wholehearted acceptance than in France, where the ground had been prepared by the work of Rousseau and the Enlightenment and where the cause of American independence had the supreme good fortune to have a representative of the genius of Benjamin Franklin. As I have already noted, Franklin possessed just that combination of cosmopolitan culture with personal originality and the exotic flavour of American democracy which appealed to the romantic liberalism of the age of Louis XVI, and his relations with philosophers and physiocrats and freemasons admitted him to the inner circle of French aristocratic society. He concealed the astuteness and *finesse* of a born diplomat under the legendary figure of patriarchal virtue and democratic simplicity, so that he was able to direct the vague idealism of philosophic liberalism towards concrete political ends. In this way the French intelligentsia came to see in America the realization of Rousseau's ideal of a state and a social order based on natural principles and inspired by a spirit of fraternity and equality. They forgot the mob law, the tarrings and featherings, and the ruthless proscription of minorities by which New England democracy had vindicated the rights of man. They forgot that the liberal culture and the spacious life of Monticello and Mount Vernon were only rendered possible by the existence of Negro slavery. They saw only the generous idealism of a Jefferson, the republican virtue of a Washington and the mellow wisdom of Franklin.

Thus the myth of the American Revolution acquired definite shape in France long before the United States themselves had acquired political form, and exerted a far stronger influence than the latter on public opinion and the development of democratic ideals in France. In the eyes of

Turgot and Mably and Reynal, of Brissot and Condorcet and Lafayette, the United States owed their importance not to what they actually were but to what they might become, and still more to what humanity might become by following their example. Said Paine:

What Archimedes said of the mechanical powers, may be applied to Reason and Liberty. *'Had we'*, said he, *'a place to stand upon we might raise the world.'* The revolution of America presented in politics what was only theory in mechanics. So deeply rooted were all the governments of the old world and so effectually had the tyranny and antiquity of habit established itself over the mind that no beginning could be made in Asia, Africa or Europe to reform the political constitution of man. But such is the irresistible nature of Truth that all it asks and all it wants is the liberty of appearing. The sun needs no inscription to distinguish him from darkness; and no sooner did the American governments display themselves to the world than despotism felt a shock and man began to contemplate redress.

PART TWO

The French Revolution

4

The Rights of Man

I n the victory of the American Revolution European
liberals saw the justification of their ideals and the realization of their hopes. It turned the current of the
Enlightenment in a political direction and infused a revolutionary purpose into the democratic idealism of Rousseau.
The young nobles, like Lafayette, who returned from
America with the prestige of heroes and apostles; the
young bourgeois, like Brissot de Warville, who looked to
America as the promised land of liberty and democratic
virtue, became the centre of a new patriotic movement
which demanded the reform of the French government
based on the democratic principle of the rights of men and
equal citizenship.

But the opposition to the *ancien régime* and the
demand for a thoroughgoing reform of the French government was by no means confined to this group of young
idealists. As de Tocqueville pointed out, the most drastic
criticisms of the old order are to be found in the preambles
to the decrees of the ministers of Louis XVI, such as
Turgot, Necker and Brienne, and before even the
Revolution had been thought of the royal government had
itself undertaken revolutionary changes, such as the abolition of the *Parlements*, the Jesuits and the guilds, which
had profoundly affected the social and economic life of the
country. Ever since the middle of the century the government had been in the hands of the friends of the philosophers such as Choiseul and Turgot and Malesherbes and
had been influenced by their ideals. But it was not only
the philosophers who were responsible for the change in the
spirit of the *ancien régime*; even more important were the

economists, the disciples of Quesnay[1] and Gournay[2] for they were not irresponsible men of letters, but serious administrators and statesmen and good servants of the king. Yet they rivalled the philosophers in their contempt for the Gothic barbarism of the *ancien régime* and in their unbounded faith in the immediate transformation of society by radical reform.[3]

No eighteenth-century ruler was more conscientious or more well meaning than Louis XVI, no European government possessed better or more intelligent ministers and officials than Turgot and Vergennes, Malesherbes and Necker, Dupont de Nemours and Senhac de Meilhan. Yet their reforming energies were frittered away in a series of false starts each of which helped to discredit the government and bring the *ancien régime* nearer to ruin. What was lacking was neither good intentions nor intelligence nor wealth (for the nation had never been more prosperous than during the reign of Louis XVI). But all these were vain in the absence of the will and energy necessary to overcome the obstacles which stood in the way of reform. In the days of Louis XIV and Colbert, France was the most powerful, efficient and well organized state in Europe, but the very success of their work was the cause of its undoing. The rambling Tudor edifice of the English constitution could be restored or changed according to the needs of each generation, but the classical structure of French absolutism did not admit of additions and alterations. The whole system centred in the person of the monarch, and if the King lacked the will and power to govern, the system ceased to function. Louis XVI had commenced his reign by undoing that one important achievement of his predecessor – the abolition of the Parlements and the

[1] Quesnay, 1694-1774, private physician to Mme de Pompadour.

[2] Gournay, 1712-59, member of the Bureau de Commerce and translator. He was the author of the famous phrase 'laissez faire : laissez passer'.

[3] Thus the elder Mirabeau wrote that it was only necessary that twelve principles, expressed in twelve lines, should be firmly fixed in the head of the Prince or his minister and carried out in detail in order to set everything right and renew the age of Solomon.

reform of the cumbrous and antiquated judicial system –
thus rendering the task of further reform almost impossible.
For the chief obstacle to financial reform was the resistance
of the privileged classes, which found a rallying point and
a centre of organization in the class of hereditary magistrates of which the *Parlements* were composed. Every
measure of administration or financial reform was opposed
by the *Parlements* in a spirit of blind conservatism which
roused the fury of Voltaire. Yet they were always ready to
justify their opposition in the name of liberty and the
rights of the subject, so that while on the one hand they
appealed to the nobility as the defenders of privilege, on
the other they appealed to the lawyers and the bourgeoisie
as the defenders of constitutional right. It was the very
class which stood in the way of reform that was loudest in
its criticism of the government and did more than the
unprivileged and the oppressed to bring about the
Revolution. It is hardly too much to say that if there had
been no *Parlement* there would have been no financial
crisis, that if there had been no financial cricis there would
have been no States General and if there had been no
States General there would have been no Revolution. The
ancien régime was destroyed by the lawyers who owed
their existence to its power and their wealth to its abuses.

There were, however, deeper sociological causes at
work in comparison with which the quarrel between the
government and the lawyers sinks into insignificance. At
the same time that the revolutionary criticism of the
Enlightenment had undermined the religious foundations
of the traditional order, the functional basis was being
destroyed by economic change. The new financial system
and the new capitalist economy were irreconcilable with
the hierarchic and authoritative principles of the *ancien
régime*. The nobility had ceased to be the natural leaders
of the nation, whose privileges were the reward of their
service to the state, as was still the case with the Prussian
officer caste. It had preserved its caste spirit and its feudal
privileges, while it had lost that control over local administration and agriculture which gave the English aristocracy

its power and social prestige. It had become merely a rich leisure class, whose chief social function was to provide a brilliant and expressive setting for the royal court. But since the heavy Baroque group of Versailles was no longer in fashion, even this function had become a sinecure, and in the eyes of public opinion the nobles were regarded as social parasites who sucked the life blood of the peasantry and battened on the resources of a discredited and bankrupt state. Above all, they had lost faith in themselves. With the exception of a few eccentrics like the Marquis de Mirabeau and the old guard of zealous Catholics, which had lost its leaders with the dissolution of the Jesuits and the death of Louis XV's eldest son and his pious wife, the nobles were in the forefront of the movement of Enlightenment. They ridiculed the Gothic barbarism of the old order. They applauded the anticlerical propaganda of the philosophers, the democratic sentiments of Rousseau and Beaumarchais, and the biting satire of Chamfort. As Ségur wrote in an often quoted passage – 'they trod lightly on a carpet of flowers towards the abyss'. And when the crash came, some of the ablest and the most exalted of them – Talleyrand, the Bishop of Autun, Herault de Séchelles, the Comte de St Simon, even Philip of Orleans, the first of the princes of the blood, were on the side of the Revolution and assisted in the work of destruction. It was only in the more remote provinces, where the nobility had preserved its traditional relations with the land and the peasants and where the influence of the Enlightenment was non-existent, that they put up a formidable resistance to the progress of revolution. Elsewhere, the proudest and most ancient aristocracy in Europe, which had its roots deep in history, fell like a rotten tree at the first blast of the storm, and resigned its rights and privileges almost without a struggle.

This triumph of the bourgeoisie over the nobility had been rendered almost inevitable by the economic changes of the last hundred years. As Barnave, the most clearsighted of the liberal leaders saw, the development of commercial and industrial capital had shifted the balance of power from the noble to the bourgeois, and though the industrial development of France had been less intense than that of England, the eighteenth century had seen an immense increase of prosperity among the middle classes, especially at the great ports like Bordeaux and Nantes, and a great development of capital investment, which already made the French *rentier* class such a considerable social power that Rivarol could assert that it was the *rentiers* who made the Revolution. Nevertheless, it was a class which had no direct political power and no recognized social status. Its very existence was inconsistent with the functional corporative structure of the old order which theoretically rejected the principle of interest as usurious and antisocial. Nor was this attitude without practical importance, for even as late as 1762 it was asserted by the economists that a third of the capitalists in France dared not invest their money profitably on account of it.[4] The new capitalist class naturally resented the antiquated ideas and unbusinesslike methods of a government of nobles and priests. They demanded a financial reform which would restore public credit and remove the danger of a default on government loans.

At last the advent to power of Necker in 1781 seemed to give them just what they wanted. For Necker was the very embodiment of the new bourgeois culture and the power of international finance – a Swiss Protestant banker who had made a fortune by successful speculation. But though Necker's administration enriched the financiers it failed to solve the financial problem. In fact the more he applied capitalist methods to government finance, the more sharp became the conflict between the interests of capital and the principles of the *ancien régime*. And so the bourgeoisie were driven by their interests as well as by their ideals to demand the political and social reforms which would give them control of taxation and a share in the government of the country. "What ought the Third Estate

[4] *La Theorie de l'Intérêt de l'Argent,* p. 180, quoted by Groethuysen, *Origine de l'Esprit Bourgeois en France,* I, p. 272. The authors of the work are said to be Goutte and Turgot.

to be?" asked the Abbé Sieyès, 'Everything. What is it? Nothing. What does it demand? To be something.'

What the bourgeoisie did not realize was that they themselves were a privileged order, and that the lawyers and men of letters who represented the Third Estate in the National Assembly had far more in common with the *noblesse de robe* or the officials than with the unprivileged masses – the true people – who belonged to a different world.

For the French peasants and workers had not been taught, like the English, to follow their landlords and employers. It had always been the policy of the French government to detach the people from the privileged classes and to maintain direct control of them through the Intendant and the Curé. They lived their own life in their communes and guilds and looked for guidance not to the nobles and the rich merchants but to the ultimate sources of all authority—the King and the Church. And hence, though they had little class consciousness in the modern sense, they had a strong national consciousness which had found expression hitherto in their loyalty to the King and their devotion to the Church. Now, however, everything conspired to shake their confidence and disturb their faith. Ever since the death of Louis XIV they had seen the higher powers at war among themselves; Jansenists and Jesuits, Church and *Parlements*, the government and the magistrates; and more recently the continual succession of reforms and counter-reforms, such as the abolition and re-establishment of the Corporations and the changes in the corn laws, together with the economic changes that produced the rises of prices and periodic crises of unemployment and food shortage, caused an increasing feeling of insecurity and discontent. There were the disorders and the revolutionary agitation of the last two years, the sinister rumours of treachery in high places, and finally the appeal of the King to the nation by the summoning of the States General and the extraordinary democratic forms of election which exceeded the demand of the reformers themselves.

All these factors combined to rouse popular feeling as it had not been roused since the days of the League. The deeps were moved. Behind the liberal aristocrats and lawyers who formed the majority of the States General, there lay the vast anonymous power that had made the monarchy and had been in turn shaped by it, and now it was to make the Revolution. To the liberal idealists – to men like Lafayette and Clermont Tonnerre, to the Abbé Fauchet and the orators of the Gironde – the Revolution meant the realization of the ideals of the Enlightenment, liberty and toleration, the rights of men and the religion of humanity. They did not see that they were on the edge of a precipice and that the world they knew was about to be swallowed up in a tempest of change which would destroy both them and their ideals. 'Woe unto you who desire the day of the Lord. It is darkness and not light. As if a man did flee from a lion and a bear met him, or went into the house and leaned his hand upon the well and a serpent bit him'; they were a doomed generation, fated to perish at first by ones and twos, and then by scores and hundreds and thousands, on the scaffold, in the streets and on the battlefield. For as the Revolution advanced it gradually revealed the naked reality that had been veiled by the antiquated trappings of royalty and tradition – the General Will – and it was not the benevolent abstraction which the disciples of Rousseau had worshipped but a fierce will to power which destroyed every man and institution that stood in its way. As de Maistre wrote, the will of the people was a battering ram with twenty million men behind it.

Nevertheless, it would be a great mistake to ignore or to minimize the importance of the intellectual factor in the Revolution, as many modern historians have done, in reaction to the idealist conceptions of Louis Blanc and Lamartine and Michelet. If we are to deny the influence of liberalism on the French Revolution we should have to deny the influence of communism on the Revolution in Russia. In fact the movement of ideas was wider and deeper in France than in Russia and had a far greater influence on the course of events. At every stage of the

Revolution, from the Assembly of the Notables in 1787 down to the fall of Robespierre in 1794, the battle of ideas decided the fate of parties and statesmen, and it was carried on not only in the National Assembly and in the meetings of the Clubs and Districts, but in the press, the streets and the cafés.

Arthur Young, who came from his quiet Suffolk village like a visitor from another world into the turmoil and excitement of revolutionary Paris, has left an unforgettable picture of the intense agitation which filled the bookshops and cafés of the Palais Royale with seething crowds both day and night during those early summer days of 1789, and he was amazed at the folly of the government in permitting this boundless licence of opinion without doing anything to counter it by the use of publicity and propaganda. The truth was that the government had to deal not with the opposition of a party but with an immense movement of social idealism which was of the nature of a religious revival. As we see from the writings of Paine and Franklin, it was a real religion, with a definite though simple body of dogmas which aspired to take the place of Christianity as the creed of the new age.

Nor was this new religious unity a purely ideal one. It already possessed its ecclesiastical hierarchy and organization in the Order of Freemasons, which attained the climax of its development in the two decades that preceded the Revolution. The spirit of eighteenth-century Freemasonry was very different from the anticlericalism of the modern Grand Orient or the conservative and practical spirit of English Masonry. It was inspired by an almost mystical enthusiasm for the cause of humanity which often assumed fantastic forms, especially in Germany, where it tended to lose itself in illuminism and theosophy. In France, however, the influence of Franklin and the Lodge of the Nine Sisters inspired the movement with a warm sympathy for the cause of liberty and political reform, which found expression in the foundation of societies like the Société des Amis des Noirs and the Constitutional Club, which were under masonic influence though directly political in aim.[5] At the beginning of the Revolution the influence of the Freemasonry permeated the ruling classes from the royal family down to the bourgeoisie, and even the Army and the Church were not exempt. How far this influence contributed to the Revolution is, however, a very controversial question. The leading figure in French Freemasonry, Philip, Duke of Orleans, was the centre of a web of subterranean agitation and intrigue which has never been unravelled, and he was certainly unscrupulous enough to use his position as head of the Grand Orient to further his schemes in so far as it was possible. What is clearer, and also more honourable, is the role of Freemasonry in generating the revolutionary optimism which inspired the aristocratic party of reform in the National Assembly. Men like Lafayette, the Vicomte de Noailles, the Duc de La Rochefoucauld, the Duc de Liancourt and the two Lameths saw in the new Revolution the fulfilment of the glorious promise of the Revolution in America. To them, and above all to Lafayette, the essence of the Revolution was to be found not in financial or even constitutional reform but in the declaration of the Rights of Man, which had marked a new era in the history of humanity. They felt like Paine, who writes as Lafayette's spokesman to the English-speaking world, that in the 'Declaration of Rights we see the solemn and majestic spectacle of a nation opening its commission, under the auspices of its Creator, to establish a government, a scene so new and so transcendently unequalled by anything in the European world, that the name of a Revolution is diminutive of its character, and it rises into a *Regeneration of Man*.'[6] 'Government founded on a *moral theory of*

[5] The former was founded by Brissot, a member of the Nine Sisters, and included Mirabeau, Siéyès, Pétion and Hérault de Séchelles. The latter included Mirabeau, Lafayette and Condorcet, as well as leaders of the parliamentary opposition such as Espremenil and Dupont, both of whom were masons. Cf. Lavisse, *Histoire de France*, IX, i, p. 307.

[6] *Rights of Man*, vol. I, p.99. (Everman ed.). Lafayette's interest in Paine's work is shown in his letter to Washington (*Memoires*, II).

universal peace, on the indefeasible hereditary Rights of Man, is now revolving from west to east by a stronger impulse than the government of the sword revolved from east to west. It interests not particular individuals but nations in its progress and promises a new ear to the human race.'[7]

Thus the French Revolution falls into place as part of a world revolution which would restore to mankind the original rights of which it had been robbed at the very dawn of history by the tyranny of kings and priests. 'Political popery, like the ecclesiastical popery of old, has had its day and is hastening to its exit. The ragged relic and the antiquated precedent, the monk and the monarch, will moulder together.'[8]

This is the same faith which inspired the speculative Freemasonry of the eighteenth century and which expresses itself in a mystical form in the early prophecies of William Blake. The Declaration of the Rights of Man made it the official creed of the French Revolution and gave the political and economic discontent of the French people a philosophical or rather theological basis on which a new social order could be based.

It is this ideological background which gave the French Revolution its spiritual force and its international significance. Without it, the Revolution might have been nothing more than a new Fronde. With it, it changed the world.

The men who did so much to bring the new gospel out of the *coulisses* of the salons and the masonic lodges on to the stage of history had no idea where their ideals would lead. Their generous illusions blinded them to the dangers in their path and they thought that the Revolution was accomplished when it had hardly begun. But none the less they played an essential part in the revolutionary drama. Lafayette, 'the hero of two worlds', on his white horse posing as a French Washington, seems an absurd or pathetic figure (Cromwell-Grandison as Mirabeau said) in com-

[7] *Rights of Man,* Part II (Introduction).
[8] *Ibid.,* Part IV.

parison with the men who were to make history, such as Mirabeau, Danton and Bonaparte. Yet had it not been for Lafayette these might never have had the chance to play their part. To the French bourgeoisie in the opening years of the Revolution, Mirabeau and Danton seemed sinister figures who were ready to play the part of a Catiline or a Clodius. And as Mirabeau was not trusted by the bourgeoisie, so neither did he trust the people. He realized the meaning of revolution and the meaning of authority, but he cared nothing for the metaphysical abstractions of the Declaration of Rights or the moral principles which inspired the liberal idealism of the moderate reformers no less than the Puritan fanaticism of Robespierre and Saint-Just. Lafayette, on the other hand, was a thoroughly respectable person, a man of high character and high principles, a good liberal and a good deist but no enemy of property and religion. And so the bourgeoisie were ready to fall in and march behind his famous white horse in defence of the cause of liberalism against both the forces of disorder and the forces of reaction.

Had it not been for this, the revolt of the Commune in July 1789 might have ended in a premature explosion which would have ruined the cause of the Revolution, for France was not ripe for democracy, and the moderate elements in the Assembly which formed the great majority saw the work of what Lafayette calls 'the infernal cabals' of the Orleanist faction behind the violence of the mob. The action of Lafayette and Bailly, however, brought the nascent revolutionary democracy of Paris into line with the bourgeois liberalism of the National Assembly. The key of the Bastille was presented by Lafayette to Washington by means of Tom Paine and its capture became transformed from an act of lawless violence into a glorious symbol of the triumph of national liberty over feudal despotism. In the same way, when the revolt of the peasants in the following months against feudalism and social war threatened to plunge the country in a social conflict which would have united the rich against the poor, the situation was saved by the idealism of the liberal aristocrats led by

Lafayette's brother-in-law, the Vicomte de Noailles, who spontaneously renounced their feudal rights in an outburst of humanitarian enthusiasm (4 August 1789).

Finally, Lafayette managed to secure a triumph for his policy of conciliation in the days of October when the forces of disorder had broken loose even more dangerously than in July. All day long he had argued and threatened and entreated, and at last, looking more dead than alive, he had been forced against his will to set out on the dreary march to Versailles in rain and darkness. Yet next day he returned in the sunlight, amidst cheering crowds and waving branches, with the King at his side and the members of the National Assembly behind him. The crisis that might have ruined him ended in his victory over both the reactionaries and the extremists. The King was forced to rally to Lafayette's programme of a democratic monarchy, while Lafayette on his side did his best to strengthen the hand of the government and restore its prestige. Order was restored. The Duke of Orleans and Marat were forced to leave the country. Mirabeau abandoned the Orleanist faction in disgust and began to make advances to Lafayette and the court. The Assembly, supported by Lafayette and the National Guard, and by Bailly and the municipality of Paris, was at last free to devote itself to the reorganization of France and the creation of a new constitution in accordance with the Rights of Man. It seemed as though the Revolution had entered a new phase, and that the alarms and excursions of the first five months would be followed by a period of peaceful consolidation. And in fact the middle period of the Constituent Assembly, from the autumn of 1789 to that of 1790, when the prestige of Lafayette was at its height, gave France a brief period of relative calm, to which liberals like Mme de Staël looked back in later years with longing and regret:

Never [she wrote] has French society been more brilliant and at the same time more serious. It was the last time, alas! that the French spirit showed itself in all its lustre. It was the last time, and in many respects also the first that Parisian society could give an idea of that intellectual intercourse which is the noblest enjoyment of which human nature is capable. Those who have lived at that time cannot help recognizing that nowhere at any time had they seen so much life and intellect so that one can judge by the number of men of talent which the circumstances of that time produced what the French would be, if they were called to take part in public affairs under a wise and sincere form of government.[9]

But if it was a time of freedom and hope, it was also a time of illusion. The Constituent Assembly went to work in a mood of boundless optimism without any regard for the facts of history or the limitations of time and place, in the spirit of their arch theorist Sieyès, who said that the so-called truths of history were as unreal as the so-called truths of religion. When their work was finished, Cerutti declared that they had destroyed fourteen centuries of abuses in three years, that the Constitution they had made would endure for centuries, and that their names would be blessed by further generations. Yet before many months had elapsed their work was undone and their leaders were executed, imprisoned or in exile. They had destroyed what they could not replace and called up forces that they could neither understand nor control. For the liberal aristocracy and bourgeoisie were not the people, and in some respects they were further from the people than the nobles and clergy who remained faithful to the old order. On the one hand there were the vast inarticulate masses of the peasantry who were ready to burn the castles of the nobles but who were often equally ready to fight with desperate resolution for their religion. On the other hand there was the people of the communes, above all the Commune of Paris. For Paris was still at heart the old city of the League and it needed no teaching from America or England to learn the lesson of Revolution. It remembered the night of St Bartholomew and the killing of Henry III, and its crowds rallied as readily to the preaching of the new Cordeliers and the new Jacobins as to that of their Catholic predecessors who led the mob against the Huguenots and held the

[9] Mme de Staël, *Considérations*.

city for five years against Henry of Navarre. Already in the days of July the people of Paris had asserted their power in unequivocal fashion and had regained their liberty by force of arms. Henceforward the people of Paris were an independent power, and a power which possessed far more political self-consciousness and revolutionary will than the people whose representatives sat in the National Assembly. It is true that in the first years of the Revolution the municipality was still in the hands of the bourgeoisie, but this was not the case with the assemblies of the districts and sections which were the real centres of political action. Here was democracy in action. Not the representative democracy of the liberal constitutionalism, but the direct democracy of the medieval communes and the Greek city states – the democracy of which Rousseau and Mably had dreamed. It was this new and terrible power which was to undo the work of the aristocratic liberals and remake the Revolution, and already in the days of the Constituent Assembly it had found its leader in Danton, and its philosopher and teacher in Marat. For the venomous and diseased little Swiss doctor, who was regarded as either a criminal or a lunatic by the respectable politicians of the Assembly, saw more clearly than they the fundamental issues of the Revolution and the bloody road that it was to travel. From the first he denounced the new constitution as the work of a privileged class and he marvelled at the way in which the workers had risked their lives to destroy the Bastille which was not their prison but that of their oppressors. He even warned the Assembly that if the bourgeoisie rejected the political rights of the workers on the ground of their poverty, they would find a remedy in the assertion of their economic rights to share in the possessions of the rich. 'How many orators boast thoughtlessly of the charms of liberty. It only has a value for the thinker who has no wish to crawl and for the man who is called to play an important part by his wealth and position, but it means nothing to the people. What are Bastilles to them? They

---

[10] 'Ami du Peuple', 30 June 1790; *Oeuvres*, ed. Vermael, p 114.

were nothing but a name.'[10] 'Where is the country of the poor?' he writes in November 1789, in reference to the question of conscription. 'Everywhere condemned to serve, if they are not under the yoke of a master, they are under that of their fellow-citizens, and whatever revolution may come, their eternal lot is servitude, poverty and oppression. What can they owe to a state which has done nothing, nothing but secure their misery and tighten their chains. They owe it nothing but hatred and malediction.'

This is very different from the optimistic liberal idealism which was the prevailing spirit in 1789-90. In fact Marat was anything but a liberal. From the first he had preached the gospel of terror and his political ideal was a popular dictatorship rather than any kind of liberal constitutionalism. But he understood the mind of the people better than Lafayette and the makers of the Constitution of 1791, and it was not liberalism but his creed of revolutionary democracy which became the creed of the Commune, the Jacobins and the Republic, in the decisive years that followed.

5

The Altars of Fear

T H E Feast of the Federation, on 14 July 1790, marks the
climax of the Liberal Revolution. It was a spontaneous
manifestation of popular feeling, a genuine act of national
consecration to the new religion of patriotism and the
ideals of Liberty, Equality and Fraternity. But it was
skilfully staged and organized by Lafayette and his party
to celebrate the triumph of his policy of national unity and
the reconciliation of the nation and the monarchy on the
platform of the Declaration of Rights.

Representations of the National Guard from the forty-
four thousand municipalities of France assembled at Paris
in the Champs de Mars, which had been transformed into
a vast open-air temple of French democracy. There, at the
great Altar of the Fatherland, Talleyrand, surrounded by
four hundred children, said mass in the presence of the
King, the National Assembly, and the armed forces of the
people, and afterwards Lafayette, followed by the National
Guards, the deputies, and the King himself, swore the oath
of federation. It was a scene of contagious enthusiasm
which communicated itself to the whole nation and it left
an ineffaceable impression on the minds of all who wit-
nessed it. The young Wordsworth, who was visiting France
for the first time at that moment, has described how the
whole land rejoiced and has given immortal expression to
the spirit of that time in the famous lines of the *Prelude*.

Yet before the union of the King and the nation, and
the harmony of the new religion of humanity with
Christianity, were solemnly consecrated in the ceremony on
the Champs de Mars, the National Assembly had passed

the law which produced a religious conflict of the most serious kind.[1]

The relations of Church and state under the old régime were so intimate that a revolution in the state inevitably affected the rights of the Church and the privileges of the clergy. But the National Assembly was not content to make these inevitable changes in the external relations of the state to the Church. It aimed at nothing less than the wholesale reconstruction of the National Church. The reformation of the Gallican Church by the National Assembly was in fact even more drastic than the Reformation of the Church in England by Henry VIII. Like the latter, the National Assembly dissolved the monasteries and abolished the religious orders; it created a National Church as in England which was in practice entirely dependent on the state, though any interference in matters of faith and dogma was disclaimed. But it went far beyond the English Reformation in its wholesale confiscation of Church property and in its revolutionary changes in the hierarchy and the ecclesiastical organization. The motive behind the whole reform is to be found in the decision that had already been taken, in the autumn of the previous year, to use the property of the Church in order to restore the solvency of the state by the issue of bonds or *assignats,* which would be repaid by the sale of Church lands. And since the state was now responsible for the payment of the clergy, it naturally treated them as public functionaries and proceeded to reorganize the Church on thoroughly Erastian lines. The ancient ecclesiastical provinces and dioceses were swept away and the map of Gallia Sancta was redrawn to coincide with that of the new France with the department as the diocesan unit. Both bishops and parish priests were to be chosen by election like other municipal officers and by the same electoral bodies – the bishops by the electors of the department and the priests by those of the district.

[1] The civil constitution of the clergy was passed by the Assembly on 12 July 1790, some additional paragraphs were added on 24 July, and it was promulgated as law on 24 August.

The Civil Constitution of the Clergy, as it was called, was mainly the work of the lawyers, like Lanjuinais and Camus, who represented the Gallican and Jansenist ideals of the old Parliamentary opposition, but behind the legalism of these narrow and unimaginative minds there was the liberal idealism which believed that the Revolution was destined to unite humanity in a new spiritual unity, and which demanded that the Church itself should become the apostle of this humanitarian gospel. This was the ideal which the Abbé Fauchet preached to enthusiastic audiences at the Palais Royal in the autumn on 1790. 'There can be only one true religion,' he declared, 'the religion which says to men "Love one another". This religion exists, it is as eternal as the law of love: it has hitherto been unrealized, and disregarded by men who have been separated by the law of descent that has ruled the world: we must show it then in its naked purity and truth and the human race attracted by its divine beauty will adore it with all its heart.'[2]

According to Fauchet, Catholics and Freemasons could unite to preach the great religious truths which found their social expression in the Revolution. But the Church of Talleyrand was as unfitted as the Freemasonry of Philippe Egalité to become the organ of this democratic mysticism. While the Civil Constitution of the Clergy was too radical to be reconciled with orthodox Catholicism, it was far too traditional to satisfy the demands of revolutionary idealism. It was not enough to bind the carcase of the old Church to the new state. What the Revolution demanded was a new civic religion which would be entirely totalitarian in spirit and which would recognize no higher duty than the service of the state.

But the time was not ripe for so radical a solution, and the Civil Constitution of the Clergy provided a convenient half-way house between Catholicism and the religion of Robespierre, which corresponded to the position of the new constitution of 1791 between the *ancien régime* and the Jacobin Republic.

[2] Aulard, *L'Eloquence Parlementaire pendant la Révolution.*

But though this liberal reformation of the Church was of little religious significance, its social and political results were of incalculable importance. In the first place, the wholesale confiscation of Church property caused immense changes in the distribution of wealth and in the economic structure of society. It dealt the final blow to the old corporative, social order and brought an immense accession of strength to the rising forces of capitalism. The class that profited most from the expropriation of the religious corporations was precisely the capitalist class – men with money to invest and with the enterprise to find profitable use for their savings. From the brokers and speculators, who made fortunes by the purchase and resale of ecclesiastical property, to the rich bourgeois, who bought the best of the abbey lands, from the village money lender and shopkeeper to the well-to-do peasant and artisan, every man with money to spend had a share in the plunder. The persistent fall in the value of the *assignats* made the operation profitable to the purchaser but disastrous to the state, and then there was created a great mass of middle-class owners of property, with an intensely individualist spirit, who were attached to the cause of the Revolution by their economic interest. At the same time the dissolution of the corporations and the laws against workers' organizations passed by the Assembly in 1790 destroyed corporative institutions among the working class and left them as an unorganized proletariat at a moment when the rise of prices and the depreciation of the currency were causing serious hardship and discontent. Nevertheless poverty and distress did not turn the workers against the Revolution. It had the opposite effect of making them more ready to listen to the propaganda of agitators like Marat, who attributed food shortages and high prices to the machinations of the court and the aristocrats, so that both the prosperity of the bourgeoisie and the poverty of the poor helped to forward the cause of Revolution and rendered it more difficult to turn back.

But it was only by degrees that the economic consequences of the revolutionary legislation were revealed.

Far more direct and obvious were the religious and political consequences of the new measures. The Civil Constitution of the Clergy almost immediately led to religious schism, and the schism in turn proved fatal to Lafayette's system of conciliation and to the whole liberal policy. The bishops, with the exception of Talleyrand and three or four others, rejected the Constitution as uncanonical, and they were followed by half the clergy and a great part of the nation. The intolerant legalism of the Assembly forced the issue on every parish priest and every village congregation by obliging the clergy to swear fidelity to the Civil Constitution on pain of deprivation.

Thus the cause of the Revolution was identified with religious schism and the Catholics who remained loyal to the Papacy and their bishops were regarded as disloyal to the Constitution. In spite of the efforts of Lafayette, Bailly and Talleyrand to maintain religious freedom, mobs organized by the extremists broke up the religious services of the nonjuring Catholics at Paris and committed brutal outrages on pious women and nuns.[3]

Nor was this outbreak of intolerance directed only against the weak: the King himself, who was a nonjuror at heart, was also a victim. When he attempted to leave Paris for St Cloud in order to receive Easter Communion privately at the hands of a nonjuring priest, his carriages

[3] These outrages have more importance than the historians of the Revolution generally recognize, as marking the beginning of religous persecution and the break between the Revolution and the constitutional liberals. We see what an effect they had in the mind of a man who was not by any means religious and was far from sympathetic towards the Catholic position in André Chenier's famous pamphlet *The Altars of Fear* which was written in a white-hot passion of indignation at the cowardly surrender of public opinion to the violence and brutality of the mob. 'We no longer build temples to Fear,' he writes. 'like the Greeks, yet never has the dark goddess been honoured by a more universal cult. The whole of Paris is her temple, and all respectable people have become her priests and every day offer to her in sacrifice their thoughts and their conscience.'

were stopped by the mob and he was forced to stay in Paris and to take part in the worship of the state Church.

In spite of Louis XVI's weakness, he was a man of deep religious feeling and this outrage to his conscience rankled in his mind and contributed more perhaps than any other factor to make him take the disastrous step of the flight to Varennes which decided the fate of the French monarchy. The sacred prestige of the French monarchy, which had survived the storms of 1789, could no longer be maintained when the King had been brought back a prisoner to his own capital and when the Assembly had been forced, if only temporarily, to usurp his sovereign powers. Nevertheless, Lafayette and the liberal majority made a brave effort to re-establish the Humpty Dumpty of constitutional monarchy. For the first time in the history of the Revolution they acted with vigour and determination against the forces of disaster. The demonstration of the clubs on the Champs de Mars a year after the Feast of the Federation was dispersed with bloodshed, Marat's journal was suppressed, and the extremist leaders, Marat, Danton, Santerre and Camille Desmoulins, were forced to go into temporary exile or hiding. But this 'Tricolour Terror', like the 'Massacre' of the Champs de Mars itself, was a very little one, and its effects were neutralized by the dissolution of the Constituent Assembly after the promulgation of the new Constitution in September 1791. By a disastrous act of abnegation the deputies had disqualified themselves for re-election, and the members of the Legislative Assembly which met on 1 October were new and untried men, mainly lawyers and professional men[4] who lacked that contact with the old governmental tradition which the leaders of the Constituent Assembly had still possessed. Moreover, in the new Assembly it was the journalists such as Brissot who took the lead, and as Albert Sorel has said it

---

[4] There were twenty-eight doctors, twenty-eight clerics, including two Protestant ministers, a number of professors and journalists, about fifty businessmen and as many landowners, and about four hundred lawyers.

was they who embittered political life with the petty jealousies of literary cliques.[5]

The new Constitution was one of the most democratic that has ever existed, in spite of the limited franchise. Not only the sovereign Assembly, but the other organs of government – local authorities of the departments and communes, judges and justices of the peace, bishops and priests and even officers of the national guard – were all elective. There was no bureaucracy, no national civil service, no centralized administrative authority. The King was a mere figurehead, his ministers were almost powerless, and the whole work of administering the country fell on the elected directories of the departments and the municipalities. As Louis XVI himself had pointed out, in his letter to the nation which he wrote before the flight to Varennes, such a system was unworkable in a country of the size and importance of France. Authority was so divided and restricted that the government no longer had any effective control over the administration, and liberty was so elaborately safeguarded that it was smothered under the burden of ceaseless elections. But outside the constitutional machinery there was growing up a new and formidable organization that possessed a ruthless will to power and was destined to inherit the authoritative and centralizing tradition of the old absolutism. Louis XVI was not remarkable for his political insight, yet he saw farther than the wise men of the Constituent Assembly when he denounced the Jacobins as 'an immense corporation, more dangerous than any of those that formerly existed', whose power must inevitably nullify the action of the government. In fact it was in the clubs and the popular societies that the Revolution found its real organs. Already in February 1791 Camille Desmoulins could describe the society as the

---

[5] *L'Europe et La Révolution*, II, p. 300. 'C'est l'avénement de ces factions d'amour propre, les plus ardentes et les plus acharnées de toutes, qui pendant plusieurs années, déchireront la France, dénatureront la Révolution et mêleront aux plus nobles luttes qui ont jamais soutenues up peuple, les plus atroces et les plus mesquines jalousies qui aient jamais divisé les hommes.'

Grand Inquisitor and the great redresser of wrongs, and already it possessed hundreds of provincial branches and affiliated societies through which it exerted an influence from one end of the country to the other.[6]

It is true that down to the great schism of 16 July 1791, when the liberal right wing, led by Barnave and the Lameths, seceded and formed the new club of the Feuillants, the Jacobins or 'The Society of the Friends of the Constitution', to give it its official title, were still moderate in their views and represented the orthodox form of revolutionary liberalism. The democrats and the *sans-culottes* found their centre in the rival club of the Cordeliers, which was responsible for the famous demonstration on the Champs de Mars in July 1791, and which embodied the spirit of revolutionary violence and terrorism. Its members included the leaders of the revolutionary Commune of August 1793, Danton, Marat, Anthoine, the butcher Legendre, Fabre l'Eglantine the poet, Camille Desmoulins and Hébert the journalists, and Fournier, 'the American', who was to play a sinister part in the September massacres. The Cordeliers never possessed the national importance of the Jacobins but they exercised an intense influence on the Parisian democracy through the Fraternal or Popular Societies founded and organized and which in turn gave the revolutionary mob its discipline and its marching orders. Thus the clubs were at once societies of propaganda and societies of action. They formed a regular hierarchy by which the doctrines and commands of the revolutionary authorities were transmitted to the people. In the words of a revolutionary journalist, every street and every village should have its club, where the decrees should be read and commented on, as the preachers do in Lent and Advent. The clubs were in fact to be the churches of the new religion. 'How was the Christian religion established?' asks a Jacobin writer. 'By the preaching of the apostles of the Gospel. How can we firmly establish the Constitution? By the mission of the

[6] There were 406 affiliated societies in May 1791.

apostles of liberty and equality. Each society should take charge of the neighbouring country districts. . . . It is enough to send an enlightened and zealous patriot with instructions which he will adapt to the locality: he should also provide himself with a copy of the Declaration of Rights, the Constitution, the Almanack du Père Gérard [by Collot d' Herbois], a good tract against fanaticism, a good journal and a good model of a pike'.[7]

In many respects the clubs had inherited and absorbed the traditions of eighteenth-century Freemasonry[8] which was itself dissolving under the storm of revolution. It possessed the same ideal of optimistic deism and claimed in the same way as the Freemasons to represent the fulfilment of the Christian ideals of fraternity, charity and morality. Their original standpoint is admirably stated by Lameth in his answer to Dom Gerle's motion that the Assembly should recognize the Catholic religion as the only authorized cult[9]. But the religion of the Jacobins was a far more definite and dogmatic theory than that of the Masons had ever been. From the first it possessed its creed in the Declaration of Rights and its scriptures on the Social Contract and it gradually developed a regular cultus and ritual centring round the Altar of the Fatherland, the Tree of Liberty, the Book of the Constitution, and addressed to deified abstractions like Reason, Liberty, Nature and the Fatherland. Although this new cult could be combined with the religion of the Church, as we have seen in the case of the Feast of the Federation, it was essentially distinct

[7] Aulard, *La Société des Jacobins.*

[8] Karmin, *L'influence du symbolisme maçonnique dans le symbolisme revolutionnaire, Revue histor. de la Révolution.*

[9] 'How is it possible', he asks, 'to doubt the religious sentiments of the Assembly. It has founded the Constitution on that consoling equality, so recommended by the Gospel. It has founded the Constitution on fraternity and the love of man. It has, to use the words of Scripture "humbled the proud"; it has put under its protection the weak and the common people whose rights were ignored. It has, indeed, realized for the happiness of mankind those words of Jesus Christ Himself, when he said "The first shall be last and the last shall be first." Aulard *L'Eloquence parlementaire.*

and potentially hostile to it. Like Christianity, it was a religion of human salvation, the salvation of the world by the power of man set free by Reason. The Cross has been replaced by the Tree of Liberty, the Grace of God by the Reason of Man, and Redemption by Revolution.

This creed was by no means peculiar to the Jacobins; it was common to all the liberal idealists from the *Illuminati* to Blake, and from Shelley to Victor Hugo. But with the Jacobin Society it acquired the external organization of a sect, with a strict discipline, a rigid standard of orthodoxy, and a fanatical intolerance of other creeds. From the first the Jacobins had thrown themselves into the struggle over the Civil Constitution of the Clergy, and the resultant conflict with the nonjuring Catholics was largely responsible for the sectarian bitterness and persecuting spirit of the Jacobin society. By degrees the Constitutional Church ceased to be the centre of the religious struggle and was itself subjected to persecution. For it was, after all, not an autonomous society but a creation of the state, and the real spiritual power behind the latter was incarnate in the Jacobin society. But already before the Jacobins had deserted the cause of the Constitutional Church,[10] they had taken the lead in demanding repressive legislation against the nonjurors and in denouncing the activities of the recalcitrant priests, while the Cordeliers and the associated popular societies took the lead in the attacks on Catholic places of worship and the mobbing of priests and nuns. And just as the first religious conflict over the Civil Constitution had alienated the King from the Constituent Assembly and led to the flight to Varennes, so the second and more intense phase, which opened in the autumn of 1791 with the law declaring 'refractory' priests to be suspect persons liable to deputation and imprisonment,

---

[10] Professor Brinton gives some interesting examples of this phase in his recent book, *The Jacobins;* for example, the president of the society at Bergerac hailed 'the election of our new [constitutional] bishop which will cause to flow through our souls the precious balm of a Constitution founded on the unshakeable basis of a holy faith' (p. 195).

brought Louis XVI into collision with the Legislative
Assembly and destroyed the possibility of any real co-
operation between the King and the Girondin leaders.

No doubt other factors contributed to the crisis. The
winter of 1791-2 saw a deterioration of the economic
situation due to a fall in the value of the *assignats* and a
rise of prices, as well as a recrudescence of peasant risings
and popular unrest in the towns, while the growing international tension, culminating in the declaration of war
with Austria in April 1792, darkened the atmosphere with
a cloud of suspicion and panic. Nevertheless, it was the
religious question and above all the refusal of the King to
sanction the second law of proscription against the priests
who refused to take the oath which brought about the final
conflict. On this one point, the King was adamant. In face
of the agitation of the clubs, the objurgation of the
Girondin orators, and the warnings of his ministers, this
stout, easy-going, undecided man showed almost superhuman courage and constancy. Nor was it the courage of
ignorance, for in his interview with Dumouriez on 18 June,
he showed that he was fully aware of the gravity of his
decision and that he fully expected that it would lead to
his death. 'I have finished with men,' he wrote 'I must turn
to God.' Two days later the mob, ten thousand strong,
organized by the extremist elements from the Cordeliers,
invaded the Tuileries and attempted to make him withdraw his veto by force. Louis was forced to undergo the
threats and gross familiarities of the crowd, which
swarmed through the palace and had the royal family at
their mercy for four hours. But the King's composure and
good humour carried him through the ordeal triumphantly
and it caused a revulsion of public opinion in his favour.
Addresses of loyalty and denunciations of the Jacobins
poured in from all over France. Lafayette returned from
the front and put himself at the head of the opposition. He
demanded that the reign of the clubs should give place to
the reign of the law and that the Jacobins should be
'annihilated physically and morally'. But the fatalistic
resignation of Louis XVI, and the Queen's dislike of

Lafayette, prevented them from accepting his bold policy of a declaration of war against the Jacobins. The Liberal constitutionalists found themselves isolated between the insurgent forces of Jacobin democracy and the passive hostility of the Catholic royalists. Actually, Lafayette's action only succeeded in throwing the Girondins into the arms of the extremists and uniting Vergniaud and Brissot with Robespierre in a campaign against the monarchy.

Thus the passions aroused by the anticlerical legislation and the royal veto divided the liberal forces and brought about the ruin of the constitutional cause. The Feuillants – the supporters of Lafayette and Dupont – joined the conservatives and the Catholics against the Jacobins, while the Girondins, who shared the same liberal principles, apart from the question of religious toleration, joined with Robespierre and the clubs in a revolutionary movement against the monarchy. On 3 July Vergniaud delivered his famous diatribe against the King, in which he painted a lurid picture of a priest-ridden monarch plotting a new St Bartholomew against the patriots, and on 11 July the Assembly declared that the country was in danger and summoned all citizens to rise in its defence. It is true that they took fright a few days later and tried to stem the tide of republican agitation. But it was already too late. The declaration of 11 July had given the leaders of the club their opportunity and the direction of events passed from the Assembly to the insurrectionary committees which controlled the assemblies of the sections and established a central organization at the headquarters of the Parisian Commune. Robespierre at the Jacobins and Danton and Manuel at the Commune were the masters of the hour, but they remained behind the scenes and left the actual preparations for the insurrection to the small fry of the clubs, especially members of the Cordeliers, Anthoine, Santerre, Collot d'Herbois, Fournier and the like. The Revolution of 10 August was the work of a determined minority which possessed an efficient organization, and the utter passivity of the constituted authorities showed the bankruptcy of the constitutional experiment. Once again, as in July 1789, the people of Paris rose against the government, but this time there was no pretence of defending the rights of the National Assembly. The authority of the Assembly disappeared with the fall of the throne and gave place to the dictatorship of the revolutionary Commune. The Legislative Assembly still existed, but it was forced to register the decisions of the Commune, and the months that elapsed between the capture of the Tuileries and the meeting of the new Assembly – the Convention – on 20 September was an anticipation of the revolutionary dictatorship that was to follow. This temporary dictatorship was embodied in three men – Danton, Robespierre and Marat – who formed a kind of unofficial triumvirate and came to stand for the new Revolution in somewhat the same way as Mirabeau, Lafayette and Sieyès had done for the earlier one. In spite of their complete diversity of character and principles, each in his own way was a representative revolutionary type—Danton, the Jacobin, bull-necked, unscrupulous, audacious, who was at his best in the confusion that followed the breakdown of authority and rallied France to the appeal of revolutionary patriotism; Robespierre, like Lafayette, the man of principles and ideals, narrow but incorruptible, the high priest of the Jacobin religion, whose inflexible will gradually imposed itself on the convention and the nation; Marat, that strange hybrid of Swiss doctor and Sardinian brigand, whose morbid fears and jealous suspicions gave him an uncanny power of appealing to the hidden forces of terror and suspicion that governed the mind of the crowd.

It was the spirit of these three men that inspired the Commune with the fierce energy which overawed the Assembly and rallied the hesitating country and army to the revolutionary ideal. For the fall of the Tuileries in itself was by no means sufficient to decide the fate of the country. The administration in the provinces and the leaders of the army were still largely in favour of the Constitution. Lafayette had attempted to raise the northeast in defence, and though he had been forced to fly the country on 19 August, royalist feeling was strong enough in other parts of the country, especially the centre and the west, to provide material for a counter-revolutionary movement. Above all, the Prussians were on the march and France, with a disorganized government and a divided army, seemed in no fit state to withstand an invasion. It was Danton, the representative of the Commune in the new Ministry, who saved the situation by his courage and energy. He overcame the defeatist spirit of his Girondin colleagues, Roland and the rest. He stiffened the resistance of the country by the despatch of commissioners to the departments with powers to raise men and munitions, purge the local authorities and influence public opinion. Above all, he tried to hold the Commune and the Assembly together, by supporting the former in its revolutionary measures – the arrest of suspects and the arming of the people – and by inspiring the latter with a spark of his energy and determination.

Nevertheless, there could be no real co-operation between an Assembly still dominated by constitutional ideals of lawyers from the Gironde, and the revolutionary violence of the Commune – between the spirit of the Gironde and the spirit of Marat. The crisis came at the end of August when the Assembly, exasperated by the overpowering behaviour of its rival and fearing for the freedom of the approaching elections, ordered the dissolution of the revolutionary Commune and the election of a new body according to constitutional forms. But the Commune refused to surrender and the Assembly hesitated to proceed to extremes. At this moment, on 2 September, the news of the investment of Verdun by the Prussians gave the Commune their opportunity. Once more, as on 9 August, the tocsin was sounded, the barriers were closed, and a desperate appeal to rally in defence of the revolution was made by the Commune to the people of Paris and by Danton in the Assembly. The same evening, parties of citizens and national guards visited the prisons and began methodically to massacre the priests and political prisoners who had been detained as nonjurors or suspects. For four days the massacres went on, while the authorities remained passive and the city and the Assembly were at once horrified and apathetic. It was the greatest killing since the day of St Bartholomew; upwards of eleven hundred persons perished, including the Princess de Lamballe, the ex-minister Montmorin, the Archbishop of Arles, two bishops, two hundred and twenty-five priests, and a number of university professors. The greater majority of the victims, however, were ordinary criminals, men, women and even children, who had no connection whatever with politics.

These atrocities were officially ascribed to an uncontrollable outburst of popular anger, but there can be no doubt that they were deliberately planned and organized by the revolutionary leaders. The primary responsibility rests with the Committee of Surveillance, of which Marat had that day become a member, and it was he who drafted the circular to the departments justifying the massacres and urging the provinces to do likewise. But behind the committee was the council of the Commune, in which Robespierre was the leading spirit, and the Minister of Justice, who was Danton. Thus the final responsibility lies with the revolutionary triumvirate, who were determined to overcome the opposition of the assembly and the hesitations of the country by this stroke. As Danton himself said to the son of the Duke of Orleans, the future King of France: 'It was my will that the whole youth of Paris should arrive at the front covered with blood which would guarantee their fidelity. I wished to put a river of blood between them and the enemy.' It was in the midst of this reign of terror that the elections to the Convention took place. Only a tenth of the electorate of Paris ventured to record their votes and the leaders of the constitutional party were paralysed by fear. Roland, the Minister of the Interior, had, it is true, made a feeble effort to assert his authority, and had declared that the government must either put a stop to these excesses or admit its impotence. But the Committee of Surveillance promptly replied by issuing warrants for the arrest of the Minister himself and several other deputies, and if Danton had not intervened it is possible that the constitutionalist leaders would have shared the fate of Montmorin and La Rochefoucauld.[11] But though Roland and Brissot were temporarily silenced they never forgave the men who had threatened them. 'Robespierre and Marat', wrote Mme Roland on 5 September, 'are holding a sword over our heads.' And again a few days later, 'This brutal demagogue [Danton] is our real ruler, we are no better than his slaves while we expect every day to become his victims.'[12]

For a moment the Girondin idealists had been made to feel the brutal reality of physical force, and henceforward they were haunted by the fear of proscription. The river of blood which had been shed to separate the Revolution from the monarchy now divided the revolutionary forces themselves and it was to grow wider and deeper until it swallowed up the opposing factions and their leaders in a common destruction.

[11] La Rouchefoucauld, the President of the Directory of the Department of Paris and one of the leaders of the liberal nobles, was arrested by the Commune at Forges and murdered on his way to Paris. The other Feuillant leaders, Dupont, Charles Lameth and Talleyrand, escaped, thanks to Danton. Thus, though Danton cannot be acquitted of responsibility for the massacres, he certainly tried to keep them within limits, whereas Robespierre, by his denunciation of Brissot and the Girondins, seems to have tried to use them to destroy his political rivals. C. J. M. Thompson, *Robespierre*, vol. 1, pp. 273-7, on the question of his responsibility.

[12] *Correspondence*, ed. Perrond, pp. 434-6.

6

The Reign of Terror

THE National Convention which met on 20 September 1792 was faced with the task of remaking the Constitution and creating a new social order. It was the first revolutionary Assembly in the sense that it was no longer bound to the traditions and institutions of the past and that there was no limit to the extent of its powers. The work of the first Revolution had collapsed with the fall of the throne and everything had to be begun anew.

In some respects the Convention was exceptionally well equipped for its task. Apart from the royalists and Feuillants it included all the leading figures of the Legislative Assembly – Brissot and Vergniaud, Gaudet and Isnard, Carnot and Cambon – as well as a few ex-members of the Constituent Assembly, such as Robespierre, Sieyès, the constituent oracle, Buzot and Barère, the Jansenist Camus, and the Protestant minister, Robert Saint-Etienne. But there were also a number of newcomers, some already famous figures of the Revolution, like Danton and Marat, Camille Desmoulins and Philippe Egalité, but most of them new men like Barbaroux and Louvet, Coutheon and Saint-Just, Collot d'Herbois and Billaud-Varennes. There were also two distinguished representatives of revolutionary internationalism, the Prussian Anacharsis Cloots and the Anglo-American, Thomas Paine.

Few assemblies in history can boast such a galaxy of famous names – orators, and writers and men of action; yet, on the other hand, few assemblies have experienced more tragic vicissitudes. With three or four exceptions all the members whose names I have mentioned and many

more came to a violent end before the Convention was
dissolved. As we have seen, the new Assembly opened
under the most unfavourable conditions. The elections had
taken place under the shadow of the massacres of
September, and even in the provinces, as Barbaroux and
Durand Maillane admitted, there was no freedom of opinion. The electoral Assemblies were controlled by the clubs
and only a very small minority of the electorate dared to
record their votes, while only a minority of the representatives who were elected actually sat in the Convention.
Yet even under these conditions, unity was not achieved.
From the beginning the Convention was divided by a bitter
feud between the parties which represented the opposing
tendencies in the revolutionary movement. On the one side
there was the Gironde, the party of Brissot and Vergniaud
and Roland, which had formed the left wing of the old
Assembly, but which had now come to stand for the ideals
of the liberal bourgeoisie and the rights of the provinces
against the revolutionary dictatorship of the Parisian
Commune. On the other, there was the Mountain, the
party of the Commune and the triumvirs, the men who
had made the revolution of 10 August and who found their
chief support in the clubs and the popular assemblies of the
urban sections. They were the party of integral revolution,
who realized the need of unity and authority and were
determined to destroy ruthlessly anything which stood in
the way of their ideals. And this ideal was above all a
religious one. They were not satisfied with political reforms
or republican institutions. They dreamt of a spiritual
republic based on moral foundations. As Robespierre wrote
in the early days of the Convention:

> Which of us would care to descend from the heights of the
> eternal principles we have proclaimed to the actual government
> of the republics of Berne, of Venice, of Holland? ... It is not
> enough to have overturned the throne; our concern is to erect
> upon its remains holy Equality and the sacred Rights of Man.
> It is not an empty name but the character of the citizens that
> constitutes a republic. The soul of a republic is virtue – that is,

love of one's country and a high minded devotion that sinks all private interests in the interest of the whole community.[1]

There can be no doubt of the sincerity of Robespierre's faith in this lofty ideal, and the consistency of his thought and the intensity of his conviction gave him an influence over the mind of his party which resembled that of a religious leader rather than that of a practical politician like Danton. It was one of the greatest paradoxes of history that this austere moralist, who had a conscientious objection to capital punishment, should have been identified in the eyes of moderates with the crimes of September and should have led the Revolution with inflexible determination into the bloody *cul de sac* of the Reign of Terror.

Already from the beginning the atmosphere of the Convention was darkened by the shadow of the Terror. It was the fear of the Terror which drove the Girondins to attack the triumvirs and the Mountain with such bitterness, while their attacks drove Danton and Robespierre back upon the support of the Commune and the policy of revolutionary violence. Yet apart from this issue, there was no reason why the two parties in the Convention should not have co-operated with one another, since they shared the same ideology. The Jacobins accepted the theories of liberalism, in spite of their intolerance and violence, and the Girondins accepted the facts of the Revolution, in spite of their constitutional principles. Both were anti-monarchist and anti-clerical, both were agreed on the trial and judgment of the king, if not on his execution, both were determined to defend the Revolution against the foreign invaders and the counter-revolutionary forces at home. But the weakness and disorganization of the French political structure had reached such a point that a conflict of any kind was dangerous, since it brought out the inherent contradiction between the liberal theory and the realities of the revolutionary situation.

[1] *Lettres à ses commettants,* in Thompson, *Robespierre* vol. 1, p. 280.

The Girondins were supreme in the National Convention; they represented, in theory, the will of the people, and they controlled the nominal government. But they had no power to enforce their authority; they possessed no executive machinery, and no real control over the local authorities. The first Revolution had transferred the control of the police from the government to the communes and departments, and the second Revolution had in its turn destroyed the power of the local administrative authorities and transformed the National Guard into the armed forces of the sections and the revolutionary Commune. The Mountain, on the other hand, had no constitutional authority, since it formed a minority in the convention, but it possessed the reality of power, since it was supported by the Parisian Commune and the sections and by the Jacobins and the popular clubs. Thus the parliamentary battle, in spite of the passion it aroused and the brilliant oratory that it displayed, was little more than a rhetorical tournament between the picked champions of the Gironde and the Mountain. The battle was decided elsewhere, in the streets and the popular assemblies, and the main forces on either side were not even represented in the Convention.

Both the parties in the Convention were almost entirely bourgeois, and consisted mainly of lawyers and officials. It is true that Danton denounced the lawyers as 'a revolting aristocracy' and that Robespierre condemned the rich, the 'culottes dorées', as enemies of republican virtue. Yet they were themselves lawyers and bons bourgeois and both maintained the sacredness of the rights of property and denounced the project of an 'agrarian law' as counter-revolutionary. In the same way the Gironde claimed to represent the opinion of the majority and to defend the rights of the provinces against the dictation of the capital. Yet they were themselves a minority faction and had joined with the Jacobins in denying political rights to royalists and religious freedom to Catholics. Behind the political conflict in the Assembly, deeper social conflicts were developing that were to carry the Revolution forward in a way that its official leaders had not intended. The rise in the cost of living, the fall in the value of the currency, the increase of unemployment, and the continual calling up of fresh levies for the army, produced a movement of popular discontent both against the government and against the profiteers and speculators who were exploiting the Revolution. The movement found a leader in the revolutionary priest, Jacques Roux, curate of St Nicolas des Champs, who had gained a following in the working-class quarters by championing the cause of the poor. Although he was not a socialist, he insisted on the necessity of realizing the social consequences of the revolution. 'Equality', he said, 'is a mere phantom as long as the rich man has the power of life and death over his fellows by monopoly. Liberty is a mere phantom so long as one class of men can starve another with impunity. Is the property of rogues more sacred than the life of man? The government has the right to declare war, that is to say, to have men massacred. How then should it not have the right to prevent those who stay at home from being starved?' The laws had been made by the rich for the rich, therefore they were cruel for the poor man, who found himself chained by laws that he was supposed to have made himself. Thus parliamentary despotism was no less terrible than that of kings, indeed it was worse, for the old government attempted to control prices in the interests of the consumer, whereas under the rule of a bourgeois assembly, there was no longer any power to keep the profiteers in check.

The new movement was in fact a reaction against the economic liberalism which was so strongly entrenched in the Constituent Assembly and in the Convention, and which found its strongest supporters among the Girondins. It was, however, not so much a socialist movement as a conservative and a counter-revolutionary one, and the enemies of Jacques Roux in the Convention were not far wrong when they compared him to the priests who led the peasant revolt in the Vendeé. It was a popular appeal from the liberal capitalism of the bourgeois republic to the traditional order of the old monarchy with its corporative organization of economic life and its strict control of prices and wages. The bourgeois democrats who composed the Jacobin opposition in the Convention had no real sympathy with this movement; in fact, even Marat, who had most in common with them, denounced Jacques Roux as a fanatic and a counter-revolutionary. But in so far as the propaganda spread among the people, they were forced to take account of it and to embody its less extreme demands in their programme in order to gain popular support, while the Girondins, on the other hand, were driven by their feud with the Commune and the men of September to become the party of order and the representatives of property and capital.

The anti-capitalist element in the struggle between the Mountain and the Gironde is shown very clearly in a Jacobin point of view reported by Dutard, the philosopher spy of the Ministry of the Interior. 'What did the Brissotins (i.e. the Girondins) want to do? he asks: '

> They wish to establish an aristocracy of the rich, of merchants and men of property, and they have refused to see that these men are the scourge of humanity, that they only think of themselves, that they only live for themselves and that they are always ready to sacrifice everything to their egotism and their ambition; that to support them just enables them to monopolize business, to pile up wealth and to govern the people with the rod of cupidity. If I had the choice I should prefer the old régime; the nobles and the priests had some virtues, whereas these men have none. What do the Jacobins say? It is necessary to put a check on these greedy and depraved men : in the old régime the nobles and priests made a barrier that they could not pass. But under the new régime there is no limit to their ambition, they would starve the people. It is necessary to put some barrier in their way, and the only thing to do is to call out the sansculottes. Wherever the mob rises you will see them run, it is enough to show them the whip and they run like children.[2]

And thus the political conflict between the Mountain and the Gironde became merged in a wider social conflict, the issue of which was largely decided by the unacknowledged

[2] W. A. Schmidt, Tableaux de la Révolution Française, vol. 2, p. 21.

influence of Jacques Roux and the 'wild men'—the *enrageés* of the working-class quarters.

Throughout the spring the situation grew more tense. While the armies were defeated, and Dumouriez turned against the republic, and the Vendée was in revolt, the two parties in the Convention denounced each other as traitors and appealed to the country against the Mountain and to the Commune against the Gironde. But when Paris rose for the third time at the end of May, it was not the leaders of the Mountain but the unknown agitators from the sections that led the revolt, and it was not the Gironde alone, but the Convention as a whole and the bourgeoisie that the Convention represented, which were the defeated parties. On 2 June the Tuileries, where the Convention met, was once more besieged by the forces of the sections, and the deputies were forced to surrender, literally at the cannon's mouth. It was now open war between Paris and the provinces, for the Girondins who escaped called the country to arms in defence of the Assembly. Denunciations of the *coup d'état* poured in from all over the country. Normandy and Brittany, Bordeaux and the Gironde, Lyons and Franche Comté, Marseilles and Toulon, all rose against the dictatorship of Paris and only twenty-two of the eighty-three departments came out on the side of the Jacobins. But once again the fragility and weakness of the liberal constitutional movement was revealed. In spite of the eloquence and the noble attitudes which made the Girondins such impressive figures on the platform, they had no capacity for leadership and the revolt of the provinces was a miserable fiasco. For the Girondin movement had no roots in the people and their control of the provincial assemblies corresponded to no social reality. If they had been able to appeal to the peasants as the Jacobins appealed to the urban proletariat, the issue might have been a very different one. But they were separated from the peasants by the barrier of class and the still deeper gulf of religion. They belonged even more than the Jacobins to the world of the Enlightenment, whereas the peasants belonged to a world that had changed little since the Middle Ages. It was the latter, however, who were the most formidable enemy that the Jacobins had to meet. While the resistance of the statesmen of the Convention, backed by the constitutional authorities of sixty departments and the richest cities of France, collapsed ignominiously, the half-armed peasants of the Vendée were defeating the armies of the republic in battle after battle.

The Vendée was a poor and backward province, without great estates or rich abbeys, but it was profoundly attached to the Church and to the missionary order founded by St Grignon de Montfort at the beginning of the eighteenth century, which had renewed popular religion in the west during the eighteenth century in somewhat the same way as the Methodists had done to popular Protestantism in Cornwall and Wales. Consequently, it was the religious question and not the political changes of the Revolution which was the cause of popular unrest. Almost the whole population supported the nonjuring church and bitterly resented the removal of their priests and the intrusion of schismatic clergy. As early as 1791 the report of the commissioners Gensonné and Gallois to the Assembly left no doubt of the seriousness of the situation, and Dumouriez, who accompanied them, spoke of the prospect of a religious civil war. But the government rejected all counsels of moderation and only increased the severity of its policy of religious repression. The fall of the monarchy deprived the Catholics of their only protection, and the King's execution was followed two months later by the ferocious law of 18 March which condemned every nonjuring priest found in the territory of the republic to death within twenty-four hours. But already the west had risen. It was the law of February, for the compulsory levy of recruits, which was the last straw. If the peasants had to fight, their enemies were not the Austrians and the Prussians, but the representatives of the hated power which had killed their King and driven out their priests. It was a spontaneous movement which owed nothing to counter-revolutionary plots or aristocratic intrigue, but sprang directly from the faith and emotion of the soul of the people. Nothing could have been more democratic than this war against the Revolution, indeed it had more of the character of a social conflict than the revolutionary movement itself. It was a war of the people against the government, of the village against the town and of the peasants against the bourgeoisie. The insurgents were for the most part simple farmers or labourers, without arms or military experience. When the church bells sounded the alarm, they would take their rosary and their guns, or pitchforks, and march on the enemy, chanting the *Vexilla regis*. And when the battle was over they would return to their fields. Although a certain number of country gentry and ex-officers, like Bonchamps and Charette, joined them, the commander of the 'Grand Catholic Army' was a pious peddlar and their boldest leader a gamekeeper, while the armies of the Revolution were commanded by a man who was the embodiment of the luxury and corruption of the old regime, the Duc de Lauzun. As one of their enemies Philippeaux said, 'They make war like *sansculottes*, while we make war like Sybarites. All the pomp of the old régime is in our camp.' And an officer who reported on the situation to the Jacobins Club at Paris asked, 'What is the good of tactics against men who fight with a rosary and a scapular in their hands and throw themselves on our artillery armed with nothing but sticks?' And he concluded that as the wretches were insensible to the language of reason, the only course was to kill them all, 'or they will kill us'.[3]

For the first time the Revolution found itself faced with a power that was deeper than its own, and if the Girondins had been in a position to ally themselves with this spontaneous explosion of regionalist sentiment, as the Jacobins used the proletarian movement in the towns, the history of the Revolution would have been a very different one. But it was the supreme fortune of the Jacobin government that its enemies were unable to unite. It was not the Jacobins, but the Girondin bourgeoisie of Nantes, which checked the triumphant progress of the peasant army of

[3] Séance of 2 August 1793.

the Vendée. The bourgeois federation of the Gironde fizzled out ingloriously, while the peasant army of the Vendée was beginning its heroic and tragic Odyssey across the Loire. Nevertheless, it is almost a miracle that the republic survived the peril that surrounded it during the critical summer and autumn of 1793. France had to meet the attack of the combined powers of Europe at a moment when her provinces were in revolt, her armies disorganized, and her government in a state of confusion. For the *coup d'état* of 2 June had not solved the contradiction between constitutional theory and revolutionary practice – between the authority of the national convention and the power of the Commune and the clubs. Danton, the representative of the victorious party, was working for peace and Garat, the Minister of the Interior, was secretly in sympathy with the Gironde, while in the sections and the clubs the party of social revolution and its leaders, Jacques and Theophile Leclerc, were taking the place of Marat, who had been assassinated by Charlotte Corday on 13 July, as the spokesmen and interpreters of popular feeling. But the time had come for the reassertion of political authority and the revolt of the Girondins had at last made the leaders of the revolution realize the need for discipline and centralization. At the very moment of the fall of the Gironde, Robespierre in a private memorandum had already laid down the main lines that the revolutionary government was to follow:

A single will is necessary [he wrote]. It must be either republican or royalist. If it is to be republican, there must be republican ministers, a republican press, republican deputies and a republican government. The internal danger comes from the bourgeois; in order to defeat the bourgeois we must rally the people. . . .It is necessary that the people should ally itself with the Convention and that the Convention must use the people. It is necessary to extend the present insurrection by degrees according to the same plan : to pay the *sansculottes* and keep them in the towns : to arm them, to inflame their anger and to enlighten them. It is necessary to exalt republican enthusiasm by every possible means.

During the last six months of 1793 this programme was carried out and the anarchic decentralization of the liberal constitution was transformed into the ruthless dictatorship of the Reign of Terror. The new republican constitution which had been rushed through the Convention in June after the *coup d'état* never left the ark of cedar wood in which it was enshrined before the table of the President of the Convention. The real constitution which gradually emerges from the revolutionary legislation of 1793 – the law of the suspects, the law of the maximum and the law of 14 Frimaire – was a very different affair. It was a totalitarian dictatorship, operating through the Committee of Public Safety, the Committee of General Security, the local revolutionary committees, and the representatives *en mission,* and embracing every detail of public and private life. It was as though the Revolution had reacted violently against all that it had done in the last four years and had suddenly returned to the centralizing traditions of the old absolutism. The Rights of Man and the principles of political and economic liberalism were banished far more effectually than they had been under Richelieu or Colbert. Nevertheless, though it was a dictatorship, it was a democratic dictatorship, not unlike that of the Soviets in its earlier phases – a dictatorship of popular committees, whose power in the last resort rested not on the army or the police but on the weapon of a mass terrorism. The dictatorship was not concentrated in a single man, even in Robespierre.

There was a multitude of dictators; every representative *en mission* possessed unlimited powers which he delegated unreservedly to all kinds of subordinate tyrants. The Revolution had passed out of the hands of the parliamentary orators and the insurgent populace and had found its instrument in men like Fouché, the sinister ex-Oratorian who passed through France like the horseman of the Apocalypse, destroying all that stood in his way, without passion and without pity.

It was by the destructive activity of such men as Fouché at Lyons, Joseph Lebon, another ex-Oratorian at

Arras, Carrier at Nantes, Tallien at Bordeaux, that the spirit of federalism and provincial independence was broken and the ideal of the One and Indivisible Republic became a terrible reality. The Jacobin dictatorship was first and foremost a war-dictatorship – a government of national defence which put the whole country under military discipline. Its spirit is in the famous law of 23 August which decreed that so long as the country was threatened with invasion the whole population was mobilized for military service. 'The young men will go to the front, married men will make munitions and transport supplies, the women will make tents and uniforms and work in the hospitals and the old men will carry on patriotic and anti-royalist propaganda.' Hence the change from the cosmopolitan idealisms of the earlier revolutionary period to an intensely militant nationalism which inspired the military policy of Carnot and which is reflected in the reports of Barère to the Convention. For the first time we see the utilization of military reports for democratic propaganda and a deliberate attempt to organize and direct public opinion and mass emotion to national ends. Nor were the wider cultural implications of this policy neglected, as we see in Barère's remarkable report on the language question (27 January 1794), which on the one hand points out the danger to national unity from the existence of linguistic minorities and, on the other, identifies the French language with the revolutionary cause and exalts it as the language of democracy and of the Rights of Man.

Thus the new phase of the Revolution, in spite of its hatred of royalty and its hostility to the past, marks a return to the tradition of Louis XIV and the *Grand Siècle*. The Committee of Public Safety stood for the impersonal authority of the nation, and, as even an enemy like de Maistre recognized, its success was essential to the preservation of national unity and power.

This, however, was only one aspect of the Jacobin regime. It was not only a government of national defence against the foreign invader, it was also a government for the defence of the Revolution against its internal enemies. 'The Republic will never be established,' declared Saint-Just, on 10 October, 'until the will of the sovereign people represses the monarchist minority and reigns by the right of conquest.... You have to punish not only the traitors but also the indifferent; you have to punish whoever is passive in the Republic and does nothing for it.... Those who cannot be ruled by justice must be ruled by the sword.' This is the principle of the Reign of Terror, which was conceived by its authors as a necessary stage of preparation and purification before a genuinely democratic regime could be inaugurated. Here a Robespierre distinguishes constitutional and revolutionary government in much the same way as the Communist distinguishes the period of proletarian dictatorship from the classless society before which it will ultimately pass away. 'The end of Constitutional government', he writes, 'is the preservation of the Republic, that of revolutionary government is its foundation. The Revolution is the war of liberty against its enemies, the Constitution is the regime of liberty, victorious and at peace.'

The work of these missionaries of terror was not confined to the repression of insurrection. They were also the missionaries of social revolution and anti-Christian propaganda. The need for national security was not the only motive behind the Terror; even more important was the discontent of the poor. The Jacobins had only succeeded in holding their own against Jacques Roux and the party of social revolution by adopting a considerable part of this programme: the enactment of the death penalty against food hoarders or tradesmen who withheld any necessary articles from immediate sale (27 July); the law of the maximum prices, which made profiteering a capital offence (29 September); and the enrolment of the unemployed in 'revolutionary armies' to execute these laws and to force the peasants to deliver their produce. These decrees averted the danger of a new Revolution, which had been hanging over Paris in the summer of 1793, and gave the Reign of Terror that proletarian and anti-bourgeois spirit which renders it in some respects the forerunner of socialism. But with the elimination of Jacques Roux, the movement fell into the hands of baser men and found its chief spokesman in Hébert, a scurrilous and unprincipled journalist who was allied with Chaumette, the procurator of the Commune, and the extremists who formed the left wing of the Jacobins and dominated the Cordeliers and the popular societies.[4]

The Hébertists were not only the party of social revolution, they were also the leaders of the anti-Christian movement which reached its height in the autumn of 1793. The Revolution was no longer satisfied with the liberal Catholicism of the Constitutional Church, it had come to regard Christianity itself as a counter-revolutionary force which must be destroyed in order to make way for the new religion of humanity. As early as 26 September Fouché had announced at Nevers that he thought it was his mission 'to substitute the worship of the Republic and natural morality for the superstitious cults to which the people still unfortunately adhere', and in the following month at Lyons he staged an elaborate anti-Christian demonstration in which a donkey wearing a cope and mitre dragged a missal and the Gospels through the streets. During the autumn all the churches in Paris were closed, Notre Dame became the Temple of Reason, and the Constitutional Bishop of Paris, Gobel, with his leading clergy, made a public renunciation of their ministry at the bar of the Convention. But the blasphemous antics of the Hébertists offended the religious sense not only of Catholics but also of the orthodox Deism of men like Robespierre. Even revolutionary opinion was shocked by their brutality and violence, and a movement of reaction against the excesses of the Terror began to make itself felt. At this moment Danton emerged from his retreat at Arcis and put himself at the head of the opposition. With all his faults, he was a bigger and more humane man

[4] Although Hébert gave his name to the party, he was neither its founder or its leader. It would be more correct to term it 'Maratist', for it claimed, not without reason, to represent the tradition of Marat and had its centre in the club of the Cordeliers.

than the other Jacobin leaders and he had been profoundly shaken by the events of the last few months. Garat, the former Minister of the Interior, who saw him before he left Paris, described him as a broken man, overcome with despair at his impotence to save the lives of the Girondin deputies. But the realization of his own danger had restored his old energy and he made a supreme effort to regain control of the revolutionary situation by taking advantage of the revelations of financial corruption and foreign conspiracy which had been made.

It was his plan to co-operate with Robespierre in his opposition to the anti-Christian campaign of the Hébertists and thus to rally him to a policy of clemency which would isolate him and Barère from the extremists of the Committee of Public Safety, Billaud-Varenne, Collot d'Herbois, and Saint-Just. In return he was prepared to support and even to reinforce the authority of the Committee of Public Safety and the central government against the Commune and the Hébertists. The campaign opened the moment he reached Paris at the beginning of Frimaire (21 November). On 1 December Robespierre launched his attack on atheism at the Jacobins and demanded a purge of the society. On 2 December Danton attacked anti-clerical intolerance in the Convention and made his famous appeal for mercy: '*Je demande qu'on épargne le sang des hommes.*' A week later Robespierre again denounced the atheists at the Jacobins, and Chaumette, the leader of the anti-Christians in the Commune, abandoned the Hébertists and rallied to Danton's policy. On 13 December Robespierre defended Danton from the attacks of the Hébertists at the Jacobins and on 14 December Danton supported the great measure of centralization which suppressed the revolutionary armies and the other provincial organs of the Terror and brought the local administration under the direct supervision of the Committee of Public Safety. But Danton's support of the government was conditional on its severing its relations with the ultra-revolutionaries, and on 22 December his supporters in the Convention brought forward a motion for the renewal of its membership which would have involved the elimination of the extremists – Billaud-Varenne, Collot d'Herbois, Hérault de Séchelles, and Jean Bon St André.

The manoeuvre came within an inch of success, for Robespierre was not insensible to the flattery of the moderates, such as Camille Desmoulins, who appealed to him in the first numbers of the *Vieux Cordelier* as the one man who could save the Republic. But the brilliant and temperamental journalist, carried away by his own eloquence, pressed the attack too far. His famous parallel between the tyranny of the Caesars and that of the terrorists ruined Danton's cautious strategy by revealing unequivocally the real implications of the moderatist campaign. The Committee of Public Safety took alarm. Collot d'Herbois returned, reeking from the mass executions at Lyons, and put himself at the head of the terrorists. The Hébertists recovered from their temporary panic and began to denounce the counter-revolutionary intrigues of Camille and Philippeaux. Above all, Robespierre realized the dangers of the schism in the Committee of Public Safety and began to detach himself from his compromising relations with the Dantonists. In his speech on 25 December (5 Nivôse) he denounced the two opposite heresies of moderation and extremism and declared his policy of adhering to the narrow path of Jacobin orthodoxy and intensifying the severity of the revolutionary tribunal. In his great speech of 5 February he proclaimed the principles of political morality on which the Jacobin dictatorship was henceforward to be based. There was no longer any room for the moral laxity of the Dantonists or the materialism and irreligion of the Hébertists. The narrow rigidity of Robespierre's temperament had transformed the liberal idealism of Rousseau into a harsh and arid fanaticism. It was not for nothing that he was the fellow-countryman of Calvin.[5] His ideal republic had something of the spirit of Calvin's Geneva, so Robespierre would deal with the liber-

[5] Calvin was born at Noyon and Robespierre at Arras.

tines of the Revolution – the new Cordeliers like Hébert and Charrette and the old Cordeliers like Danton and Camille Desmoulins. But these men had been his friends, and it was not without an effort that he resolved to sacrifice them. It required the ruthless energy of Saint-Just, the youngest and the most active member of the Committee of Public Safety, to carry his programme into action. If Robespierre was the Grand Inquisitor of the Terror, Saint-Just was its swordsman. This exquisite and aloof young man, who 'carried his head like a holy sacrament',[6] possessed a flaming energy and a cold and pitiless resolution which went through the weak and divided will of the Convention like a sword through paper.

Thus it was Saint-Just and not Robespierre who took the helm during the fatal weeks that preceded the fall of the factions and the execution of the men who had been hitherto regarded as the incarnation of the revolutionary spirit. While Robespierre withdrew on the plea of ill-health, Saint-Just launched a new social programme which was designed to rally the left and the common people to the government. The reports of Saint-Just to the Convention on 8 and 13 Ventôse (26 February and 3 March) mark the breach of the government with the bourgeoisie and its adoption of the social programme that had been first put forward by Jacques Roux and the leaders of the proletariat. They demanded the realization of the social implications of the Revolution, the complete liquidation of social elements that were opposed to the Revolution, and the transference of their property to the poor. It was only possible to found a republican order, Saint-Just declared, if social relations were brought into

[6] The phrase was coined by Camille Desmoulins in his 'Letter to Arthur Dillon', and he regarded it as the origin of the implacable enmity which Saint-Just showed towards him ever afterwards. In his last defence he wrote, 'Bourdaloue said "Molière puts me into his comedy, I will put him in my sermon". I have put Saint-Just in a comic number, and he puts me into a report for the guillotine'. *Le vieux Cordelier,* ed. Calvet, p.294.

conformity with its political principles. 'A revolution has been made in the government but it has not penetrated the social order. The government rests on liberty, the social order on aristocracy. It is impossible to have a true Revolution and a true Republic so long as the state contains the poor and the unhappy.' '*The unhappy are the powers of the earth.* They have the right to speak as masters to the governments that neglect them.' 'Let Europe know that you will no longer allow poverty or oppression on French territory, let your example bear fruit throughout the world and spread the ideals of virtue and happiness. *Happiness is a new idea in Europe.*' Here for the first time the Revolution had left the bourgeois liberalism of the eighteenth century behind it and turned its face towards a socialist ideal. Courtois was justified in asking 'where this man would have stopped in his socialism'.[7]

Saint-Just differs from Marat and Roux and Hébert in that he did not stop short at particular measures of expropriation but envisaged the possibility of a new social order which would be based on economic equality. His ideals of liberty and justice were in fact explicitly socialistic, since he held that true justice was primarily justice to the community and that it was necessary to consider not the interests of this or that individual but the interest of the state. Hence the paradox that the very speeches in which he announces the 'new idea of happiness' are at the same time an apology for the Terror. But for him the Terror is something very different from the brutal violence of *Père Duchesne*, or even from the inquisitorial heresy-hunting of Robespierre. It is an ideal Terror, 'the fire of liberty which must purify us as the dross is purged from the molten metal in the furnace', a Terror which is inseparable from the Revolution since it is of the very nature of the republic to destroy all that is contrary to it. Hence no personal consideration could be allowed to stand in the way. 'Hitherto it has been assumed that no one would dare to attack

[7] In his Report to the Convention on the events of 9 Thermidor. This is the first case I know of the use of the word socialism in its modern sense.

famous men, surrounded by a great illusion . . . . I have left all these weaknesses behind me I have seen nothing but the truth in the universe and I have spoken it.'

It was in this spirit of infallible absolutism that Saint-Just prepared the terrible reports which involved Hébertists and Dantonists, moderates and extremists, idealists and conspirators in a common destruction. The Hébertists were arrested on 13 March, and executed on 24 March. The Dantonists were arrested on 31 March and executed on 5 April. It was the greatest purge in the history of this or any other Revolution and it shook the whole revolutionary organism to its foundations. It broke the power of the Commune, the Cordeliers and the popular societies, and left the Committee of Public Safety standing alone with the Committee of General Security in the terrible isolation of absolute power. The people felt that if the men who had led them and had organized revolutionary opinion for so long were traitors, they no longer knew whom they could trust; even the memory of Marat, the patron saint of the *sansculottes,* was no longer secure, for he had been the friend of these men, and the Cordeliers, where his heart was enshrined as a sacred relic, had proved to be the centre of disaffection. The Revolution had passed from the hands of the people to those of the new revolutionary bureaucracy who wielded a power more absolute than that of any autocrat of the past. After five years of unbridled licence the reign of authority had returned and the people began once more to tremble and obey.

7

The Fall of the Mountain

T H E fall of the factions in Germinal 1794 was not merely
the victory of the revolutionary government over its political opponents, it was also the victory of Jacobin
orthodoxy over the heretics and the sceptics. Henceforward
revolutionary opinion was as rigidly organized and centralized as revolutionary government. The Jacobin society
had taken the place of the Constitutional Church as the
established Church of the republic and exercised a far
greater influence on social life than the latter had ever
done. They included in their ranks all the officials and
practically all the politically active members of the state.
Their mother society at Paris was, even more than the
Convention, the spiritual ruler of France and their thousands of local branches formed centres of propaganda and
social influence. Like the Communist Party in Russia, they
were the vital dynamic power behind the political mechan-
ism, and, like them, they derived their unity and their
authority from their faith in a social philosophy which was
also a dogmatic creed.

The chief representative and spokesman of this
Jacobin creed was Robespierre, and he owed his unique
position in the state to the way in which he had
identified himself throughout his career with the
Jacobin society and the Jacobin spirit. He was the
Pope of the new church and no pope has ever been more
determined to vindicate the supremacy of the spiritual
power. In contrast to other revolutionary leaders, like
Mirabeau and Marat and Danton, he regarded the
Revolution as essentially a moral and religious reformation.
Consequently he saw that it was not enough to adopt a

negative attitude to religious problems. The old religion
had passed with the old state, and it was necessary to give
a concrete and organic form to the spiritual ideals of the
new order. It is true that, as we have seen, the establishment of a new civic religion was implicit in the whole
development of the Revolution from the time of the Civil
Constitution of the Clergy and the Feast of the Federation
in 1790, but hitherto it had failed to attain clear expression
owing to the negative anti-clericalism which was common
to the Girondins and the Hébertists and which appeared to
Robespierre no less than to the Catholics and the members
of the constitutional Church as opposed to any religious or
moral principles whatsoever. Actually there was little
difference from the philosophical point of view between the
two schools of revolutionary thought. The only important
revolutionary thinker who made a public profession of
atheism was the arch-idealist Anacharsis Cloots, who held
that the belief in God was fatal to democracy, since the
slaves of heaven will never be free on earth. Nevertheless
Cloots's faith in humanity had a definitely religious character and he taught that the regenerate human race which
had found a centre in the new France was itself a real
divine being. 'Les attributs d'une divinité fantastique ap-
partiennent réellement à la divinité politique. J'ai dit et je
le répète que le genre humain est Dieu et que les aristo-
crates sont des athées'.[1] It is clear that there is nothing in
this attitude that is inconsistent with the idea of a civic
religion, indeed it is very similar to that of the subsequent
organizers of theo-philanthropy and the decadary cult. The
real religious conflict in the ranks of the revolutionaries was
not that between atheism and theism but between the
negative deist rationalism, which owed allegiance to
Voltaire, and the Encyclopaedists and the mystical deism
of Rousseau, which had a positive sympathy for Christian
moral ideals. And as Buonarotti, the disciple of Babeuf,
points out in his interpretation of the history of the
Revolution, these two religious ideals corresponded to two

[1] Quoted in Jaurès *Révolution Française*. ed. Mathiez, VII, p.
60.

opposite conceptions of the state and the social order which he terms respectively the *order of egotism* and the *order of equality*. Thus the rationalist anti-Christian attitude corresponds to the bourgeois liberalism which welcomed the Revolution as a means of freeing the individual from the yoke of authority and tradition, while the positive religious attitude corresponds to the attempt to realize through the Revolution a new social order based on equality, in other words the ideal of *social democracy*.

In the eyes of Robespierre and Saint-Just, the Dantonists and the Hébertists alike represented this principle of egotism, which was a kind of social atheism, and now that they had been destroyed the way seemed clear to the establishment of 'the republic of virtue'. On 18 Floréal (7 May 1794) Robespierre made his great report to the Convention, 'On the Relations of Religion and Morality to Republican Principles', which is one of the most significant documents of the revolutionary period since it provides not only the programme of the Jacobin policy of social reconstruction but an authoritative statement of the Jacobin creed. He begins by tracing in broad lines the liberal gospel of Progress on which the hopes of the Revolution were based. To Robespierre, as to Thomas Paine and to William Blake, the French Revolution was no mere political event, it was a crisis in world history which announced the birth of a new moral world and the regeneration of humanity. The modern age had seen an immense revolution in civilization which had given man the mastery over nature and had widened the horizon of human knowledge. But hitherto there had been no corresponding progress in the moral world. 'The ages and the earth have been the heritage of crime and tyranny; liberty and virtue have made a rare and intermittent appearance; Sparta gleams like a flash in tracts of darkness.' But the time had come for these fitful gleams of light to broaden out into the perfect day of democracy. 'All is changed in the physical order; all must change in the moral and political order. Half of the world revolution is already done; the other half has still to be achieved.'

What is the reason behind this uneven character in human development? It is due to the opposition of human passions and selfish interests to moral progress. Kings do not fear science and art. But they do fear 'rigid philosophers and the defenders of humanity'. The true foundations of society are morality and virtue, but existing societies are based on violence and crime. The whole principle of monarchy is essentially immoral. The essential task before the French people is the moralization of the state, and the Revolution is nothing else but the passage from the reign of crime to that of virtue. Hence France now belongs to a different moral order. It is two thousand years in advance of the rest of the world, so that the French seem to be a different species of being from the other inhabitants of Europe.

But if the Kings and their slaves are the enemies of virtue, it is also true that the enemies of virtue within the republic are their accomplices. The most dangerous of all forms of conspiracy is that which undermines the state by the corruption of public morality, and the most subtle and insidious way to demoralize society is to destroy the religious beliefs on which morality rests in the name of reason and enlightenment.

But the people were sound at heart. Where the men of letters, puffed up by the vain science of the Encyclopaedia, had lost their faith in the Revolution as they had lost their faith in God, the simple good sense of the workers had carried the cause of the Rights of Man to victory. The moral instinct of the people is the principle of its greatness. It is essential for the republic to recognize the spiritual foundation on which it rests and to use every means to restore and strengthen the beliefs without which the moral life of the people is impossible – the belief in the Supreme Being and the immortality of the soul, a religious respect for the human personality, and the sense of moral responsibility. But this does not mean any sympathy for the superstition of traditional religion. 'To recall men to the worship of the Supreme Being is to strike a mortal blow at fanaticism ... without constraint and without persecution all the sects must merge of their own accord in the universal religion of Nature.'

This religion of nature is not, however, a bare philosophical abstraction. It must be a real national religion, like the civic religions of classical antiquity, and Robespierre ends his speech with a series of concrete proposals for the establishment and organization of the new national cult. On every *decadi* throughout the year a feast is to be held in honour of the Supreme Being and of some particular moral or social object: Nature, Humanity and the Republic, Truth, Justice and Modesty, Love, Conjugal Faith and Filial Piety, Agriculture, Industry, the Benefactors of Humanity, and the Martyrs of Liberty.[2]

To the modern mind nothing would seem less likely to arouse the religious emotion of the masses than this official apotheosis of a catalogue of abstractions. But the new decadary cult is the creation of the same age which produced the neo-classical art of David and the neo-classical poetry of Schiller and the brothers Chénier; though it did not attain the intense spiritual conviction of Hölderlin's neo-paganism, it was not without an element of genuine religious feeling. The Feast of the Supreme Being, which was celebrated by Robespierre on 20 Prairial, with the assistance of the artists, musicians and poets of the republic, was not simply a pompous display of official pageantry, it was a solemn religious act which in the eyes of every good Jacobin seemed to consecrate the triumph of the cause of humanity. And on this occasion at least Robespierre's eloquence transcended the involved rhetoric of his political harangues and expressed his religious faith with complete sincerity and conviction:

Is it not He Who from the beginning of time has decreed the Republic and has ordained for all ages and for all peoples, liberty, good faith and justice?

He has not created kings to devour the human race: He has not created priests to harness us like beasts to the chariot of kings and to give the world an example of baseness and perfidy and falsehood. But He has created the universe to manifest His

[2] Cf. the project of national feasts in Saint-Just's *Institutions*.

power : He has created men to help one another, to love one another and to attain happiness by the way of virtue.

Being of beings, it is no unjust prayer that we make to Thee : Thou knowest the creatures that have come forth from Thy hands : Thou knowest their needs no less than their secret thoughts. The hatred of ill faith and of tyranny burns in our hearts with the love of justice and of our country; our blood is shed for the cause of humanity; behold our prayer, behold our sacrifice, behold the worship that we offer Thee.

It was the supreme moment of Robespierre's career, and anyone who saw him exalted by religious emotion amidst the singing crowds and the vast multitude that thronged the Champs de Mars might have supposed that the Reign of Terror was over and that a new era of fraternity and reconciliation had begun.

But Robespierre's speeches to the Convention on 27 June show that he was far from believing that the time had come to lay aside the weapon of the Terror, and that he still regarded the policy of clemency as treason to the revolutionary cause. The truth is that to Robespierre and to his followers there was no contradiction between the Reign of Terror and the religion of humanity. The guillotine was as much an emblem of the Jacobin ideal as the Tree of Liberty, and the Goddess of Liberty was a jealous deity who could not be appeased save by the traditional rite of human sacrifice. Before her image in the Place de la Révolution there was offered day by day a steadily increasing toll of victims,[3] and as time went on the executions began to lose their individual and judicial character and become impersonal and symbolic. Thus on 20 April the sacrifice might have consisted of twenty-five high magistrates of the old *Parlement*, on 8 May of twenty-eight financiers, on another of a group of great nobles, while the

[3] During the early months of the Terror the executions at Paris had numbered sixty or seventy a month, in March they rose to a hundred and twenty-two, and thenceforward they increased in terrifying proportions to 259 in April, 346 in May, 689 in June, and 966 in July (I give the figures from the printed catalogue by Picard in 1911, based on the register destroyed in 1871).

attempts on the life of Robespierre and Collot d'Herbois were followed on 17 June by a great holocaust of fifty-nine victims drawn from every class to form a representative collection of enemies of the republic.

Under such conditions it was inevitable that little regard should be paid to the case of the individual and that judges and juries should take a professional pride in making the machinery of slaughter function as smoothly and as rapidly as possible. Even if the terrible indictment of revolutionary justice that was revealed at the trial of Fouquier-Tinville needs some qualification, it is impossible to find any excuse for the wholesale destruction of innocent lives that went on week after week and month after month from the early spring to the end of July. The fact that during these last three months of the Reign of Terror, the greatest scientist, the greatest poet and the noblest woman in France – Lavoisier, André Chénier and Mme Elizabeth – were condemned for their share in imaginary plots is enough to condemn the system. The religion of virtue which Robespierre preached was responsible for as much injustice and human suffering as any of the fanaticisms or superstitions of the barbaric past. It was the religious idealism of Robespierre, that provided the moral justification for the Terror, without which it would have collapsed as it did after Thermidor. But Robespierre could not learn moderation like Fouché and Tallien and the rest, because he was more disinterested than they. He did not destroy in a spirit of wanton cruelty or violence but with the cold benevolence of an inquisitor who was determined to stamp out heresy and make men virtuous and orthodox whether they wished it or not.

Hence it is not without reason that Robespierre was regarded by his contemporaries and by posterity as the representative and embodiment of the terrorist dictatorship. Nevertheless, though his immense prestige and personal influence with the Jacobins amounted to a kind of moral dictatorship, he was never a dictator in the full sense of the word. The substance of power always remained in the hands of the Committee as a whole, so that the revolutionary dictatorship preserved its impersonal character. As Mme de Staël says, it was like the guillotine – one saw the knife rather than the hand that made it move.

Behind the high priest of the Jacobin religion whose name was on everyone's lips were the organizers and men of action, Billaud-Varenne and Collot d'Herbois, Carnot and Cambon, Jeanbon Saint-André and Robert Lindet, Couthon and Saint-Just, Barère and the two Prieurs. With the exception of Couthon and Saint-Just, these men had little sympathy with Robespierre's pretensions to moral infallibility. 'Avec ton Etre Suprême, Robespierre, tu commences m'embêter', Billaud is reported to have said, and even if he did not say it, there can be no doubt that the remark expresses the general attitude of the majority of the Committee, who were more interested in the immediate task of carrying on the work of government and national defence than with the inauguration of the religion of the Supreme Being and the moral regeneration of humanity. But whatever their faults, these men were great workers. Barère has described 'the little room in which nine members worked day and night without a President, sitting round a table with a green cloth.' 'Often after a few minutes sleep I would find a huge pile of papers in my place – reports of the operations of our enemies.' 'We wanted to give a lesson in economy. We should not otherwise have done those great deeds which astonished the world.'[4] Collot d'Herbois states that he and Billaud-Varenne had despatched no less than three hundred thousand documents to the departments and had made at least ten thousand minutes in their own hand. Nor was their activity confined to office work; not only had they practically recreated the machinery of centralized bureaucratic government, they had undertaken for the first time in history the vast task of mobilizing all the mass power and economic resources of the nation for military purposes and had thus been forced to control and regulate every

[4] Quoted by J. M. Thompson, *Robespierre*, vol. 2, p. 75.

aspect of economic life. They led armies, reorganized provinces and formed public opinion by their speeches in the Convention and at the Jacobins. Carnot led the charge which decided the Battle of Wattignies, and the demonic energy of Saint-Just drove the army of the north across the Sambré again and again in spite of successive failures.

This superhuman expenditure of energy was rendered possible by the no less abnormal state of exaltation and psychic tension in which they lived. They deliberately set themselves to force the pace – to keep the nation strung up to the highest pitch of revolutionary energy. 'As a nation can be governed with the greatest degree of weakness,' writes Saint-Just, 'so it can be governed with the highest degree of energy. Whatever pitch one sets, one can keep to, so long as one is in harmony. I believe therefore that it is necessary for us to be exalted, without excluding common sense or prudence.' It is this furious energy and this fanatical exaltation which explain the grandeur and misery of revolutionary government, and may serve in some degree to excuse the ruthless cruelty of the Committee during those summer months when the Reign of Terror reached its climax. And no one has ever made a better apology for the Terror than Billaud-Varenne, the man who was perhaps more responsible for it than any other member of the Great Committee except Robespierre, and who kept his revolutionary faith intact through twenty-five years of ignominy and exile :

The trouble with revolutions [he wrote] is that it is necessary to act too quickly; you have no time to examine; you act only in a burning fever, under the fear of not acting; under the fear of seeing your ideas miscarry. . . . The decisions for which we have been so reproached – we did not wish for the most part two days, a day, or several hours before taking them : it was the crisis alone that produced them.

In the Committee we all of us took up day and night with tired hands the immense task of leading the masses.

For two years we marched at the head of Paris against the federalized departments and the satellites of all the kings of Europe. In this sphere of tempests we could only see the common safety; we made a dictatorship without giving it any other name. *Dictatorship,* we said it in a voice that Europe could not drown : it was a dictatorship, a revolutionary government that led by violence to the Republic.

In our hands this dictatorship overcame every obstacle : we beat the Vendéens and Europe : we crushed the factions; yes, without our own divisions we would have led the country to the Republic and today a part of Europe would be politically puritan. Not one of us saw the facts, most distressing accidents no doubt, with which we have been reproached. Our eyes were fixed too high to see that the ground on which we trod was covered with blood.

We were *statesmen* : putting the safety of the cause entrusted to us above every other consideration. Do you reproach us with the means we used? But the means made that great cause to triumph. . . . Reproach us if you will but say also *They did not fail the Republic. . . .* At least we did not leave France humiliated : and we have been great in the midst of noble poverty. Have you not found all that we confiscated in the public treasury?[5]

It was this inexorable fixity of purpose, this fanatical determination to achieve these ends by any means and at any cost, which made the power of the revolutionary government. But it was also the cause of their destruction. The dictatorship of a party cannot be carried on without a certain amount of mutual toleration and subordination, and toleration was the one quality that these men entirely lacked. Robespierre and Saint-Just, Billaud-Varenne and Collot d'Herbois, were all equally sincere and equally unyielding. Billaud and Collot had yielded to Robespierre so far as to sacrifice the Hébertists, but they refused to go further and sacrifice ex-Hébertists, like Fouché and Tallien, and still more men like Vadier and Léonard Bourdon, whom they regarded as loyal servants of the Revolution. They resented Robespierre's pontifical manners and his continual assumption of moral superiority, and they suspected that by his propaganda for the Religion of Virtue and the Supreme Being he was attempting to set

[5] Billaud-Varenne, *Memoires.*

himself above the rest of the committee and secure his personal aggrandisement. Robespierre, on his part, was possessed by a monomania of jealous suspicion which led him to scent conspiracies everywhere and to regard any opposition to his personal wishes as a sign of political disloyalty. For the grandiloquent idealism of Robespierre's political philosophy was the compensation of a mind continually haunted by fear and poisoned by suspicion and hatred.

In this respect he is but too typical of the revolutionary mind, which has a pathology as well as an ideology of its own. From the days of the great fear in 1784, to the Massacres of September, from the fall of the Girondins to the Law of the Suspects, from the *Conspiration de l'Etranger* to the fall of Robespierre, fear had been the great driving force behind the Revolution. Garat gives a vivid account of the way in which the atmosphere of the Convention in its early days was poisoned by the fantastic mutual suspicions of the two parties. The Jacobins above all had exasperated this persecution complex by their ceaseless denunciations, until they saw the hand of Pitt and the counter-revolutionaries at every turn. There were some leaders of the Revolution, Danton above all, as well as lesser men like Fouché, who deliberately exploited these fears in order to rule. But it was the secret of Robespierre's power, like Marat's, that he was himself exceptionally sensitive to these irrational forces and let his imagination drive before the gale of terror. Hence when the crisis came and the differences of opinion among the members of the Great Committee could no longer be hidden, Robespierre was unable to silence his suspicions or to come to terms with his opponents. He was the slave of his own fears. He smelt conspiracy wherever he felt opposition, and so his great speech of 8 Thermidor, with its vague threats and sweeping denunciations, only served to unite the divided forces of his enemies and to bring on his own head the accumulated forces of passion and fear which had been piling up during the months of Government by Terror.

5—TGOR * *

The professional jealousy and the anti-clerical spirit of the Committee of General Security, the relentless will of Billaud, the violence of Collot d'Herbois, the practical efficiency of Carnot and Cambon, the cold unsleeping enmity of Fouché, Tallien's passion for Theresia-Cabarrus, and the selfish interests of Barras and Fréron, all combined to bring about Robespierre's downfall.

Strictly speaking, the fall of Robespierre was not a revolution, since he had never exercised a dictatorship. On the contrary, it was a victory for the revolutionary government, which had crushed an incipient movement of revolt. Nevertheless, it involved more revolutionary consequences than any event since the fall of the monarchy. It meant the end of the Reign of Terror, the fall of the Revolutionary Commune, and the closing of the Jacobins.

8

The Turning of the Tide

In the public mind Robespierre had become identified with the terrorist system, for it was he and Couthon who were responsible for the bloody law of 22 Prairial under which 1,366 victims were executed during the last seven weeks, and it was he and Saint-Just who had controlled the Bureau of General Police, which had come to be regarded as a kind of terrorist inquisition. Hence, with the fall of Robespierre, France suddenly awoke from the nightmare of the previous months and the universal reaction of public opinion carried the politicians with it. It is true that nothing could have been farther from the intentions of Billaud and Collot and the members of the Committee of General Security, who had taken such a prominent part in the attack on Robespierre, than these events. In their eyes, as Barère said in his speech to the Commune on 10 Thermidor, the events of the previous day were nothing but a disturbance which left the revolutionary government intact. But the appeal of the committees to the National Convention, and the defeat they had inflicted upon the Jacobins and the revolutionary Commune, had destroyed the equilibrium of forces on which the power of the Committee of Public Safety had been based. As soon as the Convention had been freed from its fear of the armed forces of the sections and its dependence on the second assembly that sat in the Hall of the Jacobins, it once more felt itself to be the sovereign power and the great Committee of Public Safety became in reality what it had always been in theory, a Committee of the Assembly. The experiment in pure democracy, which had always been extra-constitutional and had rested on the pikes of the sections rather than on the votes of the departments, had already been undermined by the defeat of Vincent and the Hébertists in the spring, and it could not survive the events of Thermidor. Before the Jacobins of the two committees could realize what was happening the leadership passed out of their hands into those of the 'Thermidorians', ex-terrorists like Barras and Tallien, and Fréron and Legendre, Thuriot and Merlin of Thionville, who represented the Dantonist tradition and who now found in his policy of clemency an easy path to popularity and power. 9 Thermidor was the victory of the 'Indulgents' over the Puritans, and it was followed by a relaxation of moral tension which made the maintenance of the Terror impossible. For nearly a month the Committee of Public Safety maintained a precarious hold on authority, but the decrees of 7 Fructidor (24 August) destroyed the whole system of revolutionary dictatorship by releasing the twelve executive commissions from their dependence on the Great Committee, and at the same time suppressed or reorganized the Committees of Surveillance which had been the local organs of the Terror. Soon afterwards, on 1 September, the Commune itself was finally suppressed, and on the same day the surviving Jacobin leaders, Billaud, Collot, and Barère, were forced to resign their seats on the Committee of Public Safety in the face of the growing hostility of the Thermidorian reaction.

It was in vain that the Jacobins of Marseilles called on 'The Mountain of Sinai' to thunder as of old, and Billaud-Varenne declared that the lion was not dead but only sleeping and that it would awake and destroy its enemies. They no longer had to deal with the flaccid constitutional opposition of the Feuillants and the Girodins, but with men who had been trained in the school of the Cordeliers and the revolutionary Commune, and who were able to meet the Jacobins with their own tactics of intimidation and direct action. As in the earlier days of the Revolution they had organized the mob against the aristocrats, so now Fréron and his friends organized the bourgeoisie against the Jacobins and filled the town with gangs of truculent dandies who drove the *sansculottes* off the streets. Once more, as in the old days, the cafés of the Palais Egalité (formerly the Palais Royal) were thronged with noisy crowds, and old Orleanist demagogues and bravos crawled out of their prisons and hiding places and joined in the fray. It was Sainte-Huruge who led the attack on the Jacobin Club on the night of 19 Brumaire, as he had led the mob to the Tuileries on 20 June, – 'Je suis Sainte-Huruge, c'est moi qui ai sauvé la France'. – A few days later the Convention decreed the suspension of the Jacobins, and the great club, which had been the soul of the Terror and had overcome the monarchy and the Constituent Assembly and the Girondins and the Dantonists, was ignominiously closed by Fréron and Theresia Cabarrus with only a couple of policemen to support them.

The fall of the Jacobins involved the final abandonment of the Jacobin programme of social equality and economic democracy which had inspired Saint-Just and Robespierre, and the return of the Revolution to the bourgeois liberalism of the Girondins and the Constituent Assembly. The Convention had always been bourgeois in spirit and origin, and now that it was delivered from the dictatorship of the Mountain and the dread of the revolutionary tribunal, it once more found its leaders among typical representatives of orthodox liberal constitutionalism, such as Siéyès, Larevellière-Lepeaux, Cambacérès and Boissy d'Anglas. While these were ready to ally themselves with the ex-Dantonists from the left in order to put an end to the Terror and the tyranny of the committees, they regarded themselves, not without reason, as the true guardians of the revolutionary orthodoxy which had been temporarily overclouded by Jacobin fanaticism and heresy. But in spite of its numerical strength, the centre party in the Convention had been so long accustomed to following the lead of a determined minority that they found it difficult to assert themselves. The return of the imprisoned Girondist deputies in December brought an increase of strength and confidence, and the arrest and indictment of the former leaders of the committee, Billaud, Collot and Barère, on 27 December, marks the final step in the political reorientation of the Assembly. These political changes were accompanied by a social reaction which went far deeper. The fall of the committee was followed by the liquidation of the economic regime which it had built up. For we must remember that the Terror was not only a form of religio-political repression, a Jacobin inquisition; it was also, and above all, a measure of national defence and an instrument of economic control. The law against hoarding was as fundamental to the terrorist system as the law of the suspects, and the maximum was as much a part of it as the guillotine. The unpopularity of the revolutionary dictatorship was due at least as much to the severity of its economic control as to the cruelty of its system of justice. In fact, the former was only rendered possible by the latter, and as soon as the fear of the guillotine was removed it became impossible to enforce the system of requisitions, fixed prices, and government control of markets and foreign trade. From the beginning of the reaction, on 20 September, Robert Lindet, who was responsible for economic affairs under the reign of the committee, had disavowed the social-revolutionary element in the national system of economic control and had defended it only as a necessary but temporary measure of national protection. But the economic liberalism of the majority in the Convention disapproved even of this limited form of state control, and by degrees the whole complicated system of economic regulation was abandoned, until by the end of the year the maximum itself was abolished.

But while the restoration of economic freedom benefited the farmers and the commercial classes, it was disastrous for the consumer and for the state. Prices rose, and the paper currency whose value had been partially stabilized by the drastic system of control underwent a catastrophic process of depreciation. Thus the hostility of the Jacobins and the *sansculottes* to the political reaction that followed Thermidor was reinforced by a wave of popular discontent, due to the high prices and the scarcity of food and commodities that followed the abandonment of government control. It found its natural centre in the working-class quarter of the Faubourg St Antoine, which still preserved the traditions of the revolutionary Commune, though they had lost their communal organization and the leadership of the Jacobins and the popular societies. Thus the risings of Prairial and Germinal 1795 were spontaneous popular movements which lacked the leadership of the earlier insurrectionary movements of August 1792 and May 1793. The old leaders of the sections, like Legendre, Merlin of Thionville, Bourdin de l'Oise and Tallien, were now on the side of the government, and they acted with vigour and decision. For the first time the army was called in and the forces of the Convention took the offensive against the insurgents. The defeat and disarmament of the Faubourg St Antoine and the working-class quarters completed the victory of the reaction. Throughout France the Jacobins and ex-members of the revolutionary committees were arrested and disarmed, sporadic massacres of former terrorists occurred, especially at Lyons and in the south, and the surviving leaders of the Mountain in the Convention were arrested and tried. On 17 June Romme, the scientist who had introduced the revolutionary calendar, and five other deputies, were condemned to death, and stabbed themselves as they left the tribunal with two knives that they passed from hand to hand – thus closing the episode of the Terror with an appropriately dramatic gesture.

The reaction had now gone so far that the royalists recovered their courage and the restoration of the monarchy seemed imminent. The defeat of the Jacobins had to some extent discredited the republican ideal itself. The country was thoroughly disgruntled with the government, tired of war and revolution, and still largely royalist at heart. The Thermidorian reaction and the release of the suspects had brought back into public life many ex-Feuillant and constitutional monarchists, such as Lavretelle and Mathieu Dumas, who looked back to the days of Lafayette and the constituent Assembly as representing all that was best in the revolutionary tradition. Already in February the government had conciliated royalist and Catholic opinion by opening negotiations with the royalist leader in the Vendée. All through 1794 the survivors of the Catholic and Royal army

had maintained their hopeless struggle against overwhelming odds in a devastated country. The Vendée had been
swept from end to end by the *colonnes infernaux* of
General Turreau, which were charged with carrying out the
official policy of indiscriminate massacre, while Carrier and
the revolutionary tribunal of the west seconded their efforts
with the *noyades* and firing squads of Nantes. Now Turreau
was in prison and Carrier was executed, and the indomit-
able Charette and Stofflet found themselves able to obtain
peace almost on their own terms. Religious liberty was
guaranteed, the priests were to be allowed to exercise their
ministry without hindrance, and Vendéans were even
exempted from military service and granted an indemnity
for their losses.

The pacification of La Jaunaie, following on the defeat
of the Jacobins and the ending of the Terror, strengthened
the hands of the moderates who wished to return to the
constitutional ideals of the earlier Revolution. The liberal
monarchists and the liberal republicans – the Feuillants –
and the Girondins – had far more in common with one
another than they had with the emigrés on the Right or the
Jacobins on the Left, and there seemed little reason why
they should not combine to set up a constitutional regime in
the name of the restored Dauphin. But at this moment the
unfortunate child succumbed to the effects of more than a
year's solitary confinement, and the right of succession
passed to the Comte de Provence, the future Louis XVIII,
who was the official leader of the emigrés and stood for the
restoration of the *ancien régime*.

This in itself was a serious blow to the policy of
moderation and reconciliation, and to make matters worse it
was followed by the fatal step of the expedition to Quiberon.
Republican sentiment was stimulated alike by the challenge
of foreign invasion and by its successful defeat, while the
terrible mass executions that disgraced the republican victory of 5 Thermidor undid the work of the last year and
aroused the bitter enmity of the royalists and the moderates
against the ex-terrorist leaders, Tallien, Barras and Fréron,
who had forfeited their recently acquired reputation for

clemency and conciliation, and had returned to the traditions of the Reign of Terror and the Committee of Public Safety.

It was in this threatening atmosphere that the Convention prepared the new Constitution that was intended to be the crowning achievement of its eventful career. It had seen the fall of the monarchy and the fall of the Mountain, the execution of the King and Queen, of the Girondins and the Hébertists, of Danton and Robespierre, and now its surviving members, the cautious and undistinguished men of the centre, the 'Toads of the Marsh', set themselves laboriously to build a new constitutional house of cards which would ensure the stability and permanence of the republic. The new Constitution was based on the same principles of pure liberal individualism which had inspired the Constitution of 1791 and represented a sharp reaction against the totalitarian democracy of Robespierre and Saint-Just. Its object was not to ensure the sovereignty of the general will, but rather to protect the rights of the individual and society against their natural enemy the state. It is true that the Convention did not go so far as to accept Siéyès's ingenious proposition for a legislative assembly that was not allowed to talk and a 'government' that had no executive authority, but it went even further than the Constituent Assembly in the separation of powers, the limitation of the power of the executive, decentralization, and the system of indirect election. The supreme authority was entrusted to a directory of five members chosen by the upper house from a list of fifty candidates elected by the lower house : the deputies of both houses were chosen by the electoral assemblies whose members, in turn, were elected by the primary assemblies from the citizens who possessed property producing a revenue equal to the product of two hundred days work.

It is clear that such a constitution was more likely to find support among the constitutional monarchists of the Right than from the democrats of the Left, and there can be little doubt that if it had been put into immediate operation it would have resulted in the return of a royalist majority and eventually to the return of the Bourbons. But the Convention was too deeply committed to the Revolution to envisage such a prospect with equanimity. Although the Convention was socially conservative, it was the same body which had decreed the execution of the King and the proscription of the emigrés, and the regicides realized that the restoration of the King would be their own destruction. Moreover, the sale of the confiscated lands of the Church and the emigrés had given the new bourgeoisie a vested interest in the Revolution which would also be endangered by a change of regime. Hence the Convention decided that whatever changes were made in the Constitution, there should be no change of government, and they decreed, at Tallien's instigation, that two-thirds of the new Assemblies must be elected from among the members of the existing Convention.

This unblushing attempt of an unpopular and discredited Assembly to keep itself in power against the wishes of the people it was supposed to represent exasperated conservative opinion more than all the violence and tyranny of the terrorist regime. For the first time the moderate royalists and the conservative bourgeoisie, who had hitherto passively accepted the dictatorship of the demagogues and the mob, rose in insurrection. The rising was on a larger scale and was more resolutely conducted than any of its predecessors, and if the Convention had behaved in the same way as it had done in the summer of 1793, it would certainly have succumbed. But once again the men of Thermidor came to the rescue. Barras was again put in command and acted with vigour and decision. He released and armed the *sansculottes*, who had been imprisoned after the rising of Prairial, and mustered the few available soldiers of the regular army, including a young artillery officer of the name of Bonaparte whom he had known in his terrorist days at Toulon. For the first time artillery was used methodically and drastically to meet the attack of the sections, and after a sharp engagement which cost more lives than any 'day' of the Revolution since the fall of the Tuileries, the insurgents were routed.

Vendémiaire 13 was a victory for the Convention, but it was a defeat for the policy of moderation which the Convention as a whole desired to follow. It meant that the new Constitution, which should have been the charter of bourgeois liberalism, was introduced under the auspices of Barras, a pinchback dictator who represented the most corrupt and dishonourable elements in the Orleanist and Dantonist parties, and that the new government was forced to perpetuate the traditions of religious intolerance at home and military conquest abroad which were so inconsistent with its principles. The last act of the Convention, on 24 October, was to re-enact the legislation against priests and emigrés which was a flagrant violation of the liberal creed and an undying source of ill-feeling and social unrest. Hence the government of the Directory, in spite of its constitutional appearance, remained throughout its career a kind of veiled dictatorship which maintained itself in power by a series of *coups d'état* directed against whichever party threatened to dominate the assemblies. Barras' natural penchant for intrigue led him to flirt with the idea of revolution and to cultivate relations with the remnants of the Jacobins and with partisans of social revolution like Babeuf. Carnot, on the other hand, was anxious to live down his reputation as a leading member of the Great Committee in the days of the Terror, and was ready to co-operate with the constitutionalists and even the moderate royalists in order to secure the external peace and internal order which the country needed and desired. The driving force behind the government was, however, neither Barras nor Carnot, but the Alsatian lawyer, Reubell, who in spite of his cynicism and lack of scruples was a strong republican and sincerely devoted to the national cause. He was supported by La Revellière-Lepeaux, a doctrinaire liberal who had a share in the elaboration of the new Constitution, but who was driven by his anticlerical prejudices and his blind fear of royalism to resort to dictatorial and unconstitutional measures whenever the majority in the councils showed signs of demanding a change of regime.

On the whole the directors were considerably more

capable and, apart from Barras, more honest than historians have usually admitted. Yet on the other hand it would be difficult to exaggerate their unpopularity and discredit in the eyes of public opinion both in France and abroad. They stood for the vested interests of the Revolution instead of the revolutionary ideals which the Jacobins had maintained through all the horrors of the Reign of Terror. Robespierre and Saint-Just had, no doubt, showed a far more ruthless disregard for the opinion of the majority and the lives and property of their fellow citizens, but they were ready to sacrifice their own lives as well as those of others to the realization of the new order of equality and virtue. The government of the Directory, on the other hand, seemed alike to the Jacobins and the royalists to be the exploitation of the Revolution in the interests of a class. It was the rule of the men who had profited by the Revolution, the successful politicians, the *nouveaux riches*, the men who had invested in national property and who had grown rich owing to the depreciation of the *assignats*. For the collapse of the currency is the central fact that dominates the whole social history of the period between the fall of Robespierre and the coming of Napoleon. In its own way it was an event no less revolutionary than the fall of the monarchy itself, since it completed the dissolution of the traditional corporative order and caused a wholesale redistribution of wealth and a shifting of social landmarks. Out of the whirlpool of inflation, speculation, and bankruptcy, there arose new classes and new social types which to a great extent determined the social character of nineteenth-century France. Not only did it complete the destruction of the old privileged orders which had been already ruined by the reform of the Constituent Assembly, it also ruined the rentiers and the old higher bourgeoisie, which represented so much that was best in the culture and traditions of eighteenth-century France. Their place was taken by the ruling class of self-made men who resembled the self-made men of the Industrial Revolution in their harsh individualism and their indifference to non-economic motives, while they were even more unscrupulous in their choice of means and their standards of commercial morality, since they owed their wealth not to industry and commerce but to revolution and war. As Vandal has written, 'Amidst the general disturbance of business affairs and transactions, one immense business continued to thrive – the Revolution itself', so that the vast and complicated system of interests which had grown up during seven years of Revolution had become the main factor in keeping the revolutionary movement in existence.

The resultant contrast between realities and ideals – between the Revolution as a religion and the Revolution as a business – inevitably produced the disillusionment and demoralization which marked the period of the Directory. Men asked themselves whether all the blood that had been shed, and all the sufferings and sacrifices that they had endured, had merely served to enthrone Barras and Mme Tallien in place of Louis XVI and Marie Antoinette, and to enrich the hordes of speculators and profiteers who grew rich as the people perished. But while the majority lost faith in the Revolution and took refuge in cynicism or apathy, there remained a few impenitent idealists who refused to surrender their dream of a new world and persisted in their schemes of social regeneration. They looked back with regret to the days of the Commune and the Reign of Terror, when the power of wealth was kept in check by the heavy hand of the Committee of Public Safety and when a real attempt was made to put the ideals of social democracy into practice. Many of them, it is true, had taken part in the Thermidorian reaction and had rejoiced at the fall of Robespierre, but they now realized that in destroying Robespierre they had ruined their own cause. In their eyes the true end of the Revolution was not individual liberty but social equality, and to reach this end it was necessary to go still further along the path that Robespierre and Saint-Just had traced by attacking the root of social inequality – the right of property. Thus there arose the first genuinely socialist movement of modern times – the Conspiracy of the Equals – which as Espinas insisted was no eccentric or accidental episode in the history of the Revolution but the logical culmination and the last expression of Jacobinism.

Its leader, 'Gracchus Babeuf', was, like Robespierre and Saint-Just, a native of Picardy and had acquired his communist ideals before the Revolution from Dubois de Fosseux, who was Secretary of the Academy of Arras of which Robespierre himself was a member. But his originality consists not in his adoption of the utopian communism of Morelly and Mably but in the fact that he was the first to bring this abstract communism into relation with the concrete realities of the revolutionary situation. Already in the earlier years of the Revolution he had shown his sympathy for the cause of social revolution by his relations with the leaders of the extreme Left, such as Chaumette, Fouché, Garin, and Fournier 'the American', but it was not until after Thermidor that he began to take a prominent part in the revolutionary movement as spokesman of the group of ex-Hébertists and 'Enragés' that met at the club of the Evêché. Henceforward, in spite of constant imprisonment he carried on an incessant propaganda to rouse the proletariat and to organize what he called a 'plebeian Vendée'. The phrase is significant for it marks the importance that he attached to the idea of class war. 'What is the nature of revolution?' he asked, 'and especially of the French Revolution? It is a declaration of war between the patricians and the plebeians – between the rich and the poor.'[1] This class war was not a new thing, it had always existed, it was the inevitable result of the economic inequality which is inherent in the institution of property. The revolution was simply the class war emerging into political consciousness and breaking through the legal and institutional barriers by which it had been confined.[2] And since the French Revolution had shown how fragile were these barriers and how easy it was to destroy in a moment the deep-rooted abuses of centuries, why should an exception be made in favour of the most inveterate abuse of all? The time had come to get to the root of social evil by

[1] *Le Tribun du peuple*, no. 34.
[2] *Ibid.*

destroying once for all the institution of property on which the whole edifice of injustice and inequality rests.[3]

These ideas were developed by Babeuf at a time when the economic liberalism of the ruling party in the Convention was finding expression in the abolition of the system of controlled economy and in the institution of a property franchise for the electors under the new constitution. In the eyes of liberals like Dupont de Nemours, the owners of property were the true sovereigns 'by the grace of God and of nature, of their own work and that of their ancestors, since without their consent the non-owners could not obtain either food or shelter. Such ideas were tolerable to the contemporaries of Quesnay and Turgot, who regarded the land as the only source of wealth and the peasant as the typical citizen, but they had become monstrous to men that had been ruined by the irrational catastrophes of inflation and who saw wealth not as the reward of industry but as the booty of political adventurers and unscrupulous speculators. Consequently Babeuf had little difficulty in rallying those who were still faithful to the Jacobin ideal of integral democracy to his programme of economic equality, and when the conspiracy was launched in the spring of 1796 it had the support or sympathy of almost all the surviving adherents of the Mountain, whether Robespierrists like Antonelle and Darthé and Simon Duplay, or Thermidorians of the left like Robert Lindet, the former member of the Committee of Public Safety, and Amar and Vadier of the Committee of General Security. But it was a staff without an army and the conspiracy completely miscarried.

Economic revolution was indeed the logical conclusion of the Jacobin movement and so of the Revolution itself. But ideas had lost their power. The proletariat, in spite of or because of its sufferings, had lost all faith in revolutionary action, and the bourgeoisie dreaded the return of the Terror even more than the return of the monarchy.

[3] Reply of *The Tribune of the People* to P. A. Antonelle.

PART THREE

The Impact of The Revolution

9

Religion and the Romantic Movement

THE revival of religion that followed the French Revolution was not confined to any one country or to any single Church. It was common to the Latin and Germanic peoples and to Catholic and Protestant countries. Indeed it made itself felt far beyond the limits of organized Christianity and imparted a religious tendency to social and intellectual movements of the most diverse kinds, even though they were apparently in revolt against everything orthodox and traditional, whether in the sphere of religion or morals. Christianity, which had been relegated by Voltaire to the stables and the scullery, was brought back to the court and the salon, and even those who still rejected it no longer did so in the contemptuous and cocksure manner of the man of the Enlightenment. Perhaps the most remarkable instance of this is the attitude of Auguste Comte, whose denial of all metaphysical validity to religious belief does not prevent his wholesale acceptance of the moral and ritual tradition of Catholic Christianity as one of the essential elements in the spiritual life of humanity. Thus on the one hand we have a series of religious thinkers that represents the movement of revival within the limits of organized Christianity – men such as Count Joseph de Maistre, Maine de Biran, Ballanche, and Lamennais and Lacordaire in France, Coleridge, Newman in England, Möhler and Görres in Germany, and Kierkegaard in Denmark, while on the other, there is a series of no less eminent names of men who stood outside the frontiers of Christian orthodoxy and who attempted to build up a new religious edifice on humanitarian or idealist foundations – as, for example, did St Simon, Leroux, Comte, Bazard and Guinet in France, and Fichte and Hegel in Germany.

This revival of belief in religion, or at least a respect for religion, is the more remarkable when we contrast it with the external losses that religion had suffered during the preceding period. In sheer material destruction of monasteries and churches, in confiscation of property and abrogation of privileges, the Age of the Revolution far surpassed that of the Reformation; it was in fact a second Reformation, but a frankly anti-religious one. Throughout Europe the old regime had based itself on a union between Church and state so close that any revolt against the political system involved a corresponding revolt against the established Church. Moreover, the Church was singularly ill-prepared to stand a shock of this kind. For more than half a century – first in the Bourbon kingdoms and Portugal and then in Germany and the Austrian dominions – the policy of enlightened despotism had been at work, reducing the Church to complete dependence on the secular power. The princes and statesmen who carried out this policy, Choiseul in France, Pombal in Portugal, Florida Blanca in Spain, and Joseph II and Leopold II in Austria, were themselves the disciples of the philosophers, and in some cases were animated by the same spirit that inspired Voltaire's campaign against Christianity. It was, however, not their intention to destroy the Church, but rather to make it a part of the machinery of the new bureaucratic state – and to limit its functions to that of an educational institution whose business it was to make men useful and obedient citizens. This ideal was most completely realized by the Emperor Joseph II, who set himself to rationalize and socialize the Church in his dominions with Teutonic thoroughness. No detail of ecclesiastical usage was too small to escape his meticulous regulation, and the parish priest was expected to supervise the rural economy as well as the morals of his parish. And while in Austria the Church was thus reformed by an enlightened despotism inspired by the rational and progressive ideas of eighteenth-century Freemasonry, in the rest of Germany every kind of abuse continued to reign. Nothing could be darker than the picture which the papal nuncio, Cardinal Pacca, paints of the Catholic Rhineland at the close of the century. The prince bishops lived a thoroughly secular life and squandered the resources of their sees on their courts and their mistresses. Of the electors of Mainz, the primates of Germany, Ostein was the friend of Voltaire and Erthal was the patron of the neo-pagan Heinse, and things were no better in the archdiocese of Cologne for the greater part of the eighteenth century, though the best elector, the Archduke Maximilian, was a well intentioned 'enlightened despot' of the type of his brother Joseph II.

But underneath this corruption in high places the faith of the masses remained as strong as ever. When Pacca travelled through the Rhineland, the peasants assembled in their thousands, old men and children alike, to receive the sacrament of confirmation which their own bishops had for decades neglected to administer. And when the power of the electors collapsed before the armies of the Revolution, it actually relieved the tension that existed in the German Church between the traditional Catholicism of the masses and the innovations of the enlightened prelates.

Nevertheless, the net result of the revolutionary wars and the wholesale secularization that followed the Treaty of Lunéville was to leave the Catholic Church in Germany weaker and more at the mercy of the secular power than ever before. The old order was destroyed, but there was as yet no new life to take its place; and the leaders of the clergy, like Wessenburg and Dalhberg, were still permeated with Josephite ideas.

In France at the close of the eighteenth century the situation seemed even more grave, since it was there that the rationalist propaganda of the Enlightenment had made most progress among the educated classes, and it was there that the storm of the Revolution had produced its most destructive effects. There it was not merely a question of the disendowment of the Church and its subjection to the secular power, as in the Civil Constitution of the Clergy enacted in 1790; matters rapidly reached such a pitch as to involve apostasy and wholesale persecution. Priests and nuns were executed in scores and deported and exiled in thousands. By 1795 even the constitutional clergy, which had accepted the new order and renounced all dependence on Rome, was reduced to a pitiable state: of the eighty-two bishops, some twenty-four had renounced their episcopal functions and only about fifteen were left to rally to Grégoire, the constitutional Bishop of Blois, when he attempted to restore the ruins of the Gallican Church.

Yet the very violence of the storm revealed the strength of those religious forces which the eighteenth century had ignored. The persecution itself did much to restore the prestige of religion and of the clergy by investing them with the halo of martyrdom. If it was difficult to take seriously the religion of the frivolous and the well-dressed abbés of the old regime, it was just the opposite with men like the Abbé Pinot, who mounted the scaffold like a priest going to the altar in his ecclesiastical vestments, with the words 'Introibo ad altare Dei' on his lips. The effect of such things was, in fact, just the opposite of what the Jacobins intended. Fifty years earlier, when religious conformity was enforced by law, and people were obliged to produce certificates of confession, the rising generation grew up as infidels: but now that the churches were closed and the 'refractory' clergy said mass in secret at the peril of their lives, religion took on a new lease of life and the new generation – the generation of Lamennais and the Curé d'Ars – turned to Christianity with an enthusiasm and conviction which in the preceding century had been found only among the Methodists and the Moravians.

Thus the Revolution, which was the child of the Enlightenment, also proved to be its destroyer. The philosophic rationalism of the eighteenth century was the product of a highly civilized and privileged society which was swept away by the catastrophe of the *ancien régime*. In the salons of Madame de Pompadour, Madame du

Deffand, or Madame Geoffrin, it was easy to believe that Christianity was an exploded superstition which no reasonable man could take seriously. But the same men and women felt very differently when the brilliant society that had worshipped at the shrine of Voltaire was decimated by the guillotine and scattered to the four winds. Many of them, like Chateaubriand, recovered their faith in Christianity by the stress of personal suffering and bereavement, but even those who did not recover their faith in God, lost that faith in man and in the law of progress that had been characteristic of the previous age. Rationalism flourishes best in a prosperous age and a sheltered society; it finds few adherents among the unfortunate and the defeated.

The course of the Revolution was equally fatal to the hopes of every party. It seemed as though fate had determined to explode the hollowness of any kind of idealism by the destruction of all that was best in France and by permitting only the basest elements – the Barras and the Fouchés – to survive and prosper. There were some to whom this sense of the malignity of fate came with a force of a personal revelation. One of the writers of the French emigration has described in a striking passage how this happened to him while he was making the terrible march over the frozen Zuyder Zee with the defeated English army in 1796. As he marched over the ice he felt all the illusions of the Enlightenment falling away from him under the cold light of the winter stars until he realized with a flash of blinding conviction that his life had hitherto been based on a lie. And a similar experience was had by many of the most distinguished minds of the age in many different countries.

No more terrible answer could have been given to the facile optimism of the age of Louis XVI than the twenty-five years of revolution and war from 1790 to 1815, and it is not surprising that the more sensitive minds who contemplated this long drawn out spectacle of human misery were led not only to surrender their illusions but to question the principles which had been the foundations of their whole thought. In many cases, as for instance with Senancourt, the author of *Obermann* (who is so well known to us through the poems of Matthew Arnold), or Mallet du Pan, or the young Chateaubriand, these doubts found expression in a pessimistic fatalism which left no room for human effort. There were some, however, who found in the disillusions and tragedies of the Revolution the key to a new philosophy of society dramatically opposed to those of the Enlightenment.

The chief representative of this tendency was Joseph de Maistre, one of the most original thinkers and brilliant writers of his age, and one of the most important formative influences on French thought in the early nineteenth century. His style was the fit instrument of his thought. In striking contrast to the luxuriant and cloying sweetness of Chateaubriand and his followers, it has the clash of naked steel and the strength and dexterity of the swordsman. Yet he was by no means insensitive to the new romantic appeal, as we see in rare passages like the famous and lovely description of the northern summer night and the songs of the Russian boatmen of the Neva which opens *Les Soirées de St Pétersbourg.*

Although he belonged to the pre-Romantic generation, it was not until after the Restoration that his influence was fully felt, owing to the circumstances of his life. He had spent the whole of the period from the Revolution to the Restoration in exile, and the greater part of it in Russia, as the penniless ambassador of an exiled dynasty – that of Savoy – for de Maistre, though a man of French culture and speech, was never a French citizen. But the intellectual isolation and material failure which marked his whole career only served to strengthen the almost fanatical singleness of purpose and force of conviction that characterized his thought. Beneath the exterior of a diplomat and a man of the world he hid the spirit of a Hebrew prophet, and in fact the problems that preoccupied him were fundamentally the same as those that confronted Job and Jeremiah – the problem of suffering and evil and the justification of the obscure purposes of God in history. The

men of the Enlightenment had lived on the surface of life.
They had rejected the very idea of mystery and had done
their best to eliminate and ignore everything that was
irrational and obscure; they explained the problem of
existence by denying that there was a problem to explain.
De Maistre, on the other hand, concentrated his attention
on the other side of life and made the suffering and evil of
the world the key to the understanding of it.

This insistence on the darker aspects of life earned de
Maistre the reputation of a pessimist, a fatalist and an
enemy of humanity, and it was undoubtedly shocking to
men who had been brought up in the facile optimism of
eighteenth-century thought. But de Maistre would have
replied that a philosophy which ignores these things
ignores the substance of reality. War and revolution are not
unfortunate accidents, they are the very texture of historic
change. They are not the result of the free choice of
individuals. The men who seem responsible, victors and
victims alike, are but the instruments of impersonal forces,
which move to their appointed end by paths which none
can foresee. Society is not a number of individuals who
have consciously determined to combine for the greatest
happiness of the greatest number, it is a living stream
whose surface may be partially illuminated by the fitful
light of reason but which springs from subterranean sources
and flows towards an unknown sea. In this unceasing flow,
this whirlpool of forces, in which all things pass and yet
remain the same, how is it possible to distinguish cause
from effect and means from end? And if this is the case
throughout history, it is above all so in time of revolution,
when the current of change suddenly increases its momen-
tum and sweeps away every stable institution in its path.
Wise men and fools, heroes and criminals, all contributed
to its success, whether they willed to oppose it or to turn it
to their own ends. The very men who seemed to lead and
dominate it were passive tools in the hands of events, and
they were broken and thrown aside when their hour had
passed. But this spectacle of the impotence of man to
change the course of history does not lead de Maistre to

fatalism or despair. In the mysterious force which carries men with it like straws in a torrent he sees the power of God which destroys to create and erases to write anew.

The Revolution was not an event, he wrote as early as 1794, it was an epoch in the history of humanity,[1] the birth pangs of a new age. And its real significance was not to be found in its conscious ideals, as for instance in the Declaration of the Rights of Man, which were nothing but hollow abstractions concealing the real trend of events by a sort of rationalizing mirage; it was to be found on a much deeper plane in profound spiritual changes of which the contemporary mind was still unconscious. 'What we are witnessing', he writes, 'is a religious revolution; the rest, immense as it seems, is but an appendix.'

And again:

> It seems to me that any true philosopher must choose between two hypotheses: either that a new religion is in the process of formation, or that Christianity will be renewed in some extra-ordinary way.
>
> This conjecture will only be rejected contemptuously by those short-sighted men who believe nothing is possible but what they see. What man in antiquity could have foreseen the success of Christianity in its beginnings. How then do we know that a great moral revolution has not already begun?[2]

De Maistre regarded the Revolution as a cleansing fire in which the forces of evil were employed against their will and without their knowledge as agents of purification and regeneration; and as he believed that France and the French monarchy would emerge stronger than ever after the Terror and the wars of the Revolution had accomplished their work; so, too, he believed that the destruction of the Gallican Church and the ecclesiastical system of the old regime at the hands of the enemies of religion was a necessary step towards the restoration of the unity of Christendom and the freedom and universality of the Church. This ideal was in fact the dominant preoccupation

[1] Letter to Mme de Costa, in G. Goyan, *La Pensée religieuse de J. de Maistre,* p. 88.
[2] *Considerations sur la France.*

of Joseph de Maistre's mind from his young days when he urged Ferdinand of Brunswick, in 1781 at the time of the Masonic Congress of Wilhelmsbad, to transform the order of Freemasons into a society for the union of the Churches, down to his old age when he was the intellectual leader of Ultramontanism. For however intransigent his views, and however inflexible his orthodoxy, de Maistre was always ready to recognize the 'signs of the times', whether in Freemasonry and Illuminism, or in the French Revolution or the Holy Alliance, whose weaknesses he fully realized. All of them were in his eyes phases of the great religious revolution which was inevitable and already far advanced. "It is their function to melt the metal, afterwards the status will be cast."[1] 'All our plans', he wrote in 1809, 'vanish like dreams. I have preserved as much as I could, the hope that the faithful will be called to rebuild the edifice, but it seems to me that new workers advance in the profound obscurity of the future and that Her Majesty Providence says, "Behold I make all things new".'[2]

Of course de Maistre's philosophy of history is not quite so Christian as this. It has a certain Hindu or Buddhist element in it – history is governed by an impersonal law of retribution or Karma. Every evil will or act produces an inevitable fruit of suffering – the innocent may pay for the guilty, but history shows that the full payment must be made. The only way out of this circle of guilt and suffering is to be found in detachment and in the voluntary acceptance of suffering.

And this view of history as a superhuman process which transcended the aims and ideas of the men who were apparently the makers of history was to influence all the thinkers of the next generation in both camps – on the one hand the founders of socialism and Positivism like the St Simonians, especially Bazard and Comte, on the other the founders of liberal Catholicism, like Lamennais and his school, and of the Catholic conservatives like Donoso Cortes.

[1] Letter to Count De Vallaise, October 1815 (Oeuvres XIII, pp. 163-4.)   [2] *Oeuvres*, X, 405-6.

But in his own time de Maistre was an isolated figure standing between 'two worlds, one dead, the other powerless to be born'. He belongs neither to the eighteenth nor the nineteenth century, neither to the Enlightenment nor to the Romantic movement. But though this simple and austere gentleman of the old regime has little in common with the undisciplined, emotional, unstable spirit of Romanticism, there is a curious parallelism between his thought and that of the leaders of the Romantic movement. This parallelism is seen most clearly in the essay on *Europe or Christendom* composed by the young Novalis in 1798, only two years after de Maistre's *Considerations on France*. In spite of his Protestant origins, Novalis exalts the religious ideal of the Middle Ages and condemns the Reformation for its sacrilegious attempt to divide the indivisible Church and to imprison religion within political frontiers. Like de Maistre, he regards the Reformation as the source of rationalism and free thought, which found its culmination in the work of the Revolution. But at the same time he sees in the Revolution the dawn of a new era and shares de Maistre's belief that the signs of the times pointed to a great spiritual renewal which would bring Europe back to religious unity. All the early Romantics were inspired by the same consciousness of an imminent spiritual revolution, all of them were enemies of the Enlightenment and admirers of medieval Catholicism, and many of them, such as Friedrich and Dorothea Schlegel, Adam Müller, Zacharias Werner, Franz von Baader, Görres and Clemens Brentano found their spiritual home in the Catholic Church.

It would of course be a mistake to ignore the existence of a Protestant element in the movement. Schleiermacher, perhaps the chief formative influence on Protestant religious thought in the nineteenth century, was a friend of the Schlegels and was closely associated with the origins of the movement, while at a later date the most original Protestant thinker of the nineteenth century, the Dane, Søren Kierkegaard, was a true Romantic in spite of his isolation and his hostility to everything for which Schleiermacher stood.

Nevertheless contemporary opinion was not unjustified in regarding Romanticism as a Catholicizing movement. The tendency is to be seen most clearly years before the conversion of the Schlegels in the writings of early Romantics like Wackenroder and Novalis, who never themselves became Catholics and whose admiration was in no way inspired by propagandist motives.

I have already referred to Novalis' remarkable panegyric of medieval Catholicism and his criticism of the Reformation, and in the same way Wackenroder in 1797 initiated that return to the religion of the Middle Ages through the art of the Middle Ages which became so typical of the Catholic revival in the nineteenth century. This Catholicizing tendency, which was denounced by Heine and the young German school as mere reactionary sentimentalism, did much to render Romanticism unpopular in the later nineteenth century, as we see for example in the well-known volumes of George Brandes, *The Romantic Movement in Germany* (1873), which for all their ability are biased by an almost sectarian bitterness. In reality, however, the religious element in Romanticism, whether Catholic or non-Catholic, goes much deeper than the superficial aesthetic appeal. It has its roots in the fundamental principles of the movement, which differed not merely aesthetically but also metaphysically and psychologically from those of both seventeenth-century Classicism and eighteenth-century Rationalism.

Behind the change in literary taste and aesthetic appreciation there lies a profound change of spiritual attitudes: an attempt to enlarge the kingdom of the human mind by transcending the limits of ordinary consciousness. Human consciousness is a little circle of light amidst the surrounding darkness. The classicist and the rationalist keep as close to the centre of the circle as possible and order their life and their art as though this little sphere of light was the universe. But the romantic was not content with this narrow sphere. He sought to penetrate the secret of the great reality that is hidden behind the veil of darkness and preferred the twilight regions that fringe the verge of consciousness to the lighted house of reason. Thus the most profound expression of the romantic spirit is to be found, not in the Byronic cult of personality or the aesthetic gospel of Keats' *Ode to a Grecian Urn*, but in Novalis' *Hymns to the Night* with their mystical exaltation of death. There is in fact a definite connection between romanticism and mysticism, for religious mysticism tends to express itself in the form of romantic poetry, as in the poems of St John of the Cross, while literary romanticism at its highest aspires to the ideal of religious mysticism, as in the case of Novalis and Blake.

In the same way the victory of classicism at the end of the seventeenth century was intimately connected with the defeat of mysticism and was followed by what Henri Brémond, in his great work on the history of religious sentiment in France, calls 'la retraite des mystiques'. Throughout the eighteenth century mysticism was exiled from the world of higher culture, and the religion of society became more and more arid and rationalistic. Mysticism took refuge among the sects – Quakers and Quietists, Moravians and Methodists, Swedenborgians and Illuminists – or in Catholic Europe among the common people where it produced saints like Benedict Joseph Labré, who seems as out of place in the age of Enlightenment as an Indian fakir in a London club. This artificial separation of the higher culture from the deeper forms of religious experience has been described by Coleridge in the remarkable passage of the *Biographia Literaria* in which he acknowledges his own debt to the mystics.

The Romantic movement had its roots deep in this religious underworld, and M. Viatte, in his learned work on *The Occult Sources of Romanticism*, has shown how manifold were the lines of communication which lead from Boehme and the seventeenth-century mystics through Swedenborg and St Martin and Lavater to the Romantics of the early nineteenth century. On the one hand this stream flowed back to its original source in the Catholic Church, while on the other it mingled with the stream of political and social change and inspired the new revolutionary movements with a spirit of religious enthusiasm and apocalyptic hope.

But the most remarkable product of this subterranean current of religious influence is to be found in England in the person of William Blake, for here we see it, as it were, in its pure state before it had incorporated into the social and religious movements of the new age, and when it was still unaffected by contact with the outer world. Blake was considerably senior to the rest of the Romantics not only in England but on the continent also. He belonged to the generation of de Maistre rather than to that of Wordsworth and Coleridge and Novalis. Like de Maistre he was a lonely thinker, a spiritual exile, though his place of exile was not in distant Russia on the banks of the Neva, but by the waters of the Thames at Lambeth. Like de Maistre, he was a prophet who saw historic events *sub specie aeternitatis*, as in that strange picture of Pitt as the angel who rides on the wings of the storm, 'ordering the Reaper to reap the Vine of the Earth and the Plowman to plow up the Cities and Towers'. But here the resemblance ends. In their principles and politics the two men are antitheses. De Maistre, the devout Catholic and the royalist noble, the apostle of moral order and social authority, Blake a man of the people, a heretic of heretics and a revolutionary of revolutionaries, an apostle of anarchy and antinomianism; moreover, while de Maistre is still faithful to the classical tradition in the clarity of his style and the firm logic of his thought, Blake surpasses all the Romantics in formlessness and obscurity. He knows nothing of logic and cares nothing for consistency. He regards reason as the enemy of spiritual vision and science as the tree of death. He builds up vast cloudy mythologies without troubling to explain their meaning or to reconcile their contradictions. Yet whoever has the patience and the imagination to follow him through his strange visionary world will gain a more direct insight into the process of spiritual change that was taking place under the surface of European consciousness than is to be found in any other writer. For Blake, unlike the other Romantics, emerges directly from the religious underworld and has little contact with the literary movements of his age. He was brought up a Swedenborgian, and although he soon diverged from the narrow line of Swedenborgian orthodoxy, he continued to live his spiritual life in the world of sectarian theosophy – the world of Lavater and St Martin and Willermoz. Yet at the same time his revolutionary sentiments brought him into contact with the free-thinkers and political reformers of the London Corresponding Society and the Friends of Liberty, such as Paine and Godwin, and his earlier prophetic writings are directly inspired by his enthusiasm for the cause of the Revolution. This earlier phase of his thought seems at first sight to be not merely unorthodox but anti-Christian and anti-religious. Religion is the 'Web of Urizen', the evil God of the Old Testament who enslaves mankind under the iron laws of morality. The Messiah of the new gospel is the Spirit of Revolution, Orc, 'The Son of Fire' who 'stamps the strong law to dust and scatters religion abroad to the four winds as a torn book'. Thus the one evil is repression: 'He who desires and acts not, breeds pestilence ... Energy is Eternal Delight ... For everything that lives is holy, life delights in life: because the soul of sweet delight can never be defiled.'

This gospel of anarchy expressed in Blake's earlier writings has much in common with the creed of the romantic liberals and Utopian socialists such as Godwin, Shelley, and the young Fourier, but it is already distinguished from the orthodox revolutionary creed by its hostility to Rationalism and to the empirical philosophy of the eighteenth century. Blake would have agreed with de Maistre in his view that 'contempt of Locke is the beginning of wisdom', and both assailed the philosophy of Bacon with the same animosity, as in Blake's epitaph on Bacon:

O reader behold the Philosopher's grave :
He was born quite a Fool and he died quite a Knave.

Moreover the progress of the Revolution disillusioned Blake no less than the other Romantics. The mood of the earlier prophetic books gradually changes from rapturous hope in the new dawn to an atmosphere of apocalyptic terror and gloom, culminating in the *Song of Los* with its grim frontispiece showing a headless figure brooding over a desolate landscape.

During the period of his stay at Felpham, 1800 to 1803, at about the same time that German Romanticism was turning towards Christianity, Blake went through a spiritual crisis which transformed his religious attitude. He speaks in 1804 of having been for twenty years 'a slave bound in a mill among beasts and devils'. 'I have indeed fought through a hell of terrors and horrors (which none could know but myself) in a divided existence; now no longer divided nor at war with myself I shall travel on in the strength of the Lord God, as Poor Pilgrim says.'

These twenty years correspond approximately with his revolutionary period which followed his Swedenborgian youth, when he came under the influence of the Enlightenment as represented by Godwin and Priestley and Paine. Now he returned to Christianity, though it was a strange theosophical Christianity that had more in common with Boehme and St Martin than with any kind of Christian orthodoxy.

'I know of no other Christianity and no other Gospel', he writes, 'than the liberty both of body and mind to exercise the Divine Arts of Imagination – Imagination the real and Eternal World of which this Vegetable Universe is but a faint shadow and in which we shall live in our Eternal or Imaginative Bodies when these Vegetable Mortal Bodies are no more.'[1]

But Blake's imagination is no subjective human faculty; it is the Creative and Eternal Logos. 'Imagination is the Divine Vision, not of the World, nor of man, nor from man – as he is a natural man.'[2] Nor do his pantheism

---

[1] *Jerusalem,* Preface to the Christians.
[2] Note to Wordsworth.

and antinomianism cause him to shut his eyes to the problem of evil and the necessity of moral effort. He was equally hostile to the facile optimism of the Radicals, with their cult of enlightened self-interest, and to the callous indifference of Church and state.

> O divine Saviour [he prays], arise
> Upon the Mountains of Albion as in ancient time! Behold!
> The Cities of Albion seek thy face: London groans in pain
> From Hill to Hill, and the Thames laments along the valleys:
> The little villages of Middlesex and Surrey hunger and thirst:
> The 28 cities of Albion stretch their hands to thee.
> Because of the Oppressors of Albion in every City and Village.
> They mock at the Labourer's limbs: they mock at his starv'd children:
> They buy his Daughters: that they may have power to sell his Sons:
> They compel the Poor to live upon a crust of bread by soft mild arts:
> They reduce the Man to want then give with pomp and ceremony:
> The praise of Jehova is chanted from lips of hunger and thirst.[3]

This intense sensitiveness to the sufferings of the poor distinguishes the religion of Blake from the orthodox Christianity of the age. If his ideal of creative imagination and spiritual intuition resembles that of the German Romantics, his devotion to social justice has more in common with the utopian socialism of Fourier and the St Simonians. He is an isolated figure standing alone between the religious underworld of the sects and the secular world of contemporary art and literature, and leaving no disciples to develop his thought in one direction or the other.

Nevertheless he is a significant figure, because he reflects in a highly individual and independent form the spiritual conflict which underlies the social changes of the age and which resulted from the insurgence of the spiritual forces that had been repressed by the rationalism and moralism of the Enlightenment. This movement took two different forms: on the one hand, as in the Catholic revival

[3] Jerusalem.

on the continent, and subsequently in the Oxford Movement in England, it was a movement of return to the tradition of historic Christianity – a Catholic Renaissance – which went back behind the Enlightenment and behind the Reformation to the religious faith and the religious art of medieval Christendom; and on the other hand it was a movement of innovation and change, which proclaimed the advent of a new religion in harmony with the spirit of the new age, in the style of the new Christianity of the St Simonians, Comte's Religion of Humanity, or Mazzini's Religious Nationalism. Nevertheless, in spite of the apparent opposition of these two forms they are far more closely connected than one would suppose. The religious liberalism of Lamennais developed from the religious traditionalism of de Bonald and de Maistre, Comte was a disciple of the same school and borrowed the forms of his religion of the future from the religion of the past, while some of the chief apostles of the Religion of Progress, such as Pierre Leroux and Buchez, advanced through the new Christianity to the old. Religion failed to reconquer and reunite European civilization as de Maistre and the Christian Romantics had hoped; but on the other hand, it recovered its vitality and once more asserted itself as an autonomous force in European culture. In comparison with the eighteenth century, the nineteenth century, especially the first half of it, was a religious age.

10

Europe and the Revolution

THE fact that the French Revolution should have attempted the complete reorganization of the social order which we have seen in the preceding chapters shows how vast were the forces that had been set loose by the impact of the new ideas of the Enlightenment. It is true that France had been ripe for great social and political changes. The government was weak and inefficient, the financial system was breaking down, social discontent was rife, above all the ruling classes, which had been the strength of France in earlier centuries, had been converted by the policy of Louis XIV into an ornamental class of courtiers, which had lost its real function and its contact with the nation and had become a parasitic body which could be removed without much detriment to the national life. But all this does not suffice to explain the cataclysm that actually took place. Conscious social and political revolutions, which we in modern Europe take for granted, are extraordinarily rare in history. They occur only when a civilization has lost its spiritual unity and is undergoing a process of internal transformation.

French society lost its inner cohesion with the breakdown of the Counter-Reformation culture, which in its Gallicanized form had inspired the civilization of the *Grand Siècle,* and the Revolution was an attempt to recreate this unity on the basis of the new eighteenth-century thought.

This explains its international importance, for wherever the dissolvent action of the French movement of Enlightenment had penetrated, there the Revolution awoke a sympathetic response and the armies of the Revolution were received as liberators. It seemed for a time as though Europe would recover on this new basis the unity that she had lost since the end of the Middle Ages, especially when Napoleon brought his supreme gifts as conqueror and organizer to the consolidation of the revolutionary achievement.

For although the French Revolution was a political movement, it was not merely a political movement like the English Revolution of 1688 or even the American Revolution of 1776. It was also a spiritual revolution, no less than the Reformation had been, the realization in practice of that religion of humanity which had been the creation of eighteenth-century thought. Behind the armies of the Revolution and those of Napoleon stood the Declaration of the Rights of Man and the revolutionary idealism. The great series of military conquests achieved by France was made in the name of humanity and liberty and equality. It starts off with the solemn renunciation by France of the right of conquest (in the Constituent Assembly's decree of 22 May 1790), and it came to be regarded as a crusade for the liberation of humanity against the allied forces of despotism, as is shown in the decrees of 19 November and 15 December 1792, which declared war on the privileged classes and offered help to all the people who would rise against their oppressors.

Even the enemies of the Revolution, like de Maistre, saw in it something more than human. He wrote in 1796: 'It has been said with truth that the Revolution leads men rather than men lead the Revolution. Those who have established the republic have done so without willing it and without knowing what they are doing; they have been led by events, instruments of a power that knew more than they did themselves.'

Now Napoleon himself was the greatest of these instruments of the Revolution. It is true that in a sense he undid the work of the Revolution, so far as democratic institutions are concerned. But he preserved the essential features of the new order – civil equality, the abolition of social privilege, intellectual and religious liberty, and the

furtherance of science and education, and established them
on a practical basis. As he himself said: 'The romance of
the Revolution is over; we must now commence its history.
We must have eyes only for what is real and practical in
the application of principles, and not for the speculative
and hypothetical.'

If from one point of view his militarist imperialism
seems the antithesis of the pacifist liberalism of 1789, on
the other hand he was the great organizer of what the
Revolution had achieved.

Through him France became the first modern national
state with the first rationalized code of law and the first
system of unified national state education. Through him
again this state became the instrument for the moderni-
zation of the whole European political and social order.

He was the heir at once of Danton and of Louis XIV,
and his work represents the readaptation of the political
tradition of the European state to the needs of the new
culture. Under his rule the national glory of the age of
Louis XIV was renewed, and at the same time the scientific culture of the Age of the Enlightenment was crowned
by the work of the great French scientists, such as Laplace
the astronomer, Lamarck the biologist, Bertholet the
chemist, and Champollion the founder of Egyptology.

Above all, it was Napoleon who swept away the
picturesque absurdities of the Holy Roman Empire and the
three hundred minor states of Germany which represented
the debris of feudalism and the relics of the wars of
religion. In their stead he incorporated western Germany,
the Low Countries and Italy into a single state and thus
prepared the way for the modern development of Europe
and the rise of the new national states.

Nevertheless, this great achievement was vitiated by the
spirit of predatory militarism which accompanied it. It was
not an organic unity, but an artificial structure created by
a *condottiere* of genius. Napoleon was a great political
rationalist and his rationalization of the Revolution
destroyed the revolutionary idealism that had been the
dynamic spiritual force behind it. The armies of Napoleon

might free the peasants of Germany from the burdens of an antiquated feudalism, but they were the servants of an alien imperialism, not the missionaries of international freedom.

But there was a still more fundamental weakness in the Napoleonic empire. There was an inherent contradiction between its cosmopolitan culture and the militant nationalism of the revolutionary armies that had created it. And so the very strength of the influence of French ideas tended to arouse similar ideals of nationalism among the subject peoples. Thus the very men who had been the most ardent disciples of the French Revolution became the leaders and apostles of the nationalist reaction. This is most obvious in Germany in the case of men like Arndt, Görres and Fichte, but we also see it at a still earlier period in Italy with Alfieri and later in England, as for example in Wordsworth's pamphlet on the Convention of Cintra, and in Spain with the national movement against Napoleon. Hence, as Sorel pointed out, the Revolution itself supplied the arms that they were to destroy it, for the principles invoked by allies in the war of liberation were based on the revolutionary ideal of national self-determination rather than on the strict legitimist ideals of the counter-revolution. Consequently, to the Germans and the Spaniards and the Spanish Americans the War of Liberation had an almost revolutionary character. It was not so much a war against the Revolution as an adaptation of the revolutionary ideal to their own national needs and traditions. As a result of this, the German liberals of the nineteenth century looked back at the Arndt and the War of Liberation, and the Spanish liberals to the Cortes and the Constitution of Cadiz, in much the same manner as French liberalism of the nineteenth century looked back to the French Revolution and the principles of 1789.

Consequently the downfall of the Napoleonic empire and the restoration of the Bourbons in France and Spain and Sicily were far from marking the end of the revolutionary movement. The revolutionary spirit survived and found expression in the new nationalist movements which spread like an epidemic from one end of Europe to the other. The whole period from 1789 to 1848 (or indeed from 1770 to 1870) is an Age of Revolution. First came the great revolutionary storm of the 1790s which swept over western Europe like a torrent, destroying the French monarchy and the Holy Roman Empire and 'casting the kingdoms old into another mould'. And hardly had this torrent been dammed and canalized into the imperial order of the Napoleonic system before a fresh storm arose which destroyed the elaborate structure that Napoleon had built up and brought back the old monarchies, which for a time seemed to be the champions of the rights of nations. But no sooner was the Restoration achieved than the new European settlement began to be disturbed by a fresh series of revolutionary national movements which spread from the circumference of Europe to the centre till it culminated in the general explosion of 1848.

On the other hand, had Napoleon been successful in the task that he set himself, western Europe would have returned to the political and cultural unity from which its development had begun in the Carolingian Age. This grandiose idea was shattered not only by its irreconcilability with the principle of nationality, but even more owing to its collision with the one great power which had remained unaffected by the Revolution.

For while the culture of the continent was being transformed by the movements that we have described, English society had been developing on its own lines in a different direction. Abroad, the eighteenth century had been an age of political and social centralization, in England the Revolution of 1688 had destroyed both the political power of the crown and the social influence of the court, and had transferred the real control of the state to the rural classes. Eighteenth-century England was a republic of squires, administered by an oligarchy of great landowners, such as the Russells, the Cavendishes and the Pelhams. Local government was carried on not by the official agents of the central government, as in France, but by the justices of the peace, all of them members of the same landowning class, which also controlled Parliament and the national administration. It was an almost patriarchal system of government, without police or bureaucracy, in which the machinery of the centralized modern state was almost entirely lacking. Such a society might seem essentially unprogressive and almost of the nature of a reaction to medieval feudal conditions. But the agrarian predominance was compensated by a great development of the mercantile and moneyed interest. From Stuart times national prosperity had come to depend largely on trade and navigation, and their importance was fully recognized at the time of the Revolution settlement. The new system of national finance, which was marked by the creation of the Bank of England and the national debt, strengthened the influence of the moneyed interest.

Throughout the eighteenth century the progress of trade went hand in hand with the movement of colonial expansion, and it was the mercantile interests that led to the building up of the overseas empire, above all in India.

The political supremacy of the landed aristocracy did not arouse the opposition of the middle classes, since they had ample scope for their energies elsewhere, and since there was no sharp division, as on the continent, between the upper and the middle classes. The younger sons of the gentry went into business, and success in trade made it possible for the merchant to purchase an estate and himself become a member of the privileged class. In a society which was so decentralized and which offered such wide opportunities for individual initiative, there was little room for ambitious projects of social and political reform, such as occupied the energies of continental thinkers. The whole culture of the age was individual and domestic. It expressed itself in the Georgian domestic architecture, with its sober taste and practical comfort, and in the art of the great English portrait painters, with their delineation of personal character and individual aristocratic types.

The spirit of the continental movement of Enlightenment certainly existed in England. But it was confined to a limited circle, to men like Pope and

Bolingbroke, Hume and Gibson, Horace Walpole and Lord
Chesterfield, who were oten in closer touch with foreign
society than with the minds of their own countrymen. The
ordinary Englishman cared little for foreign culture and the
abstract principles of the philosophers. Liberty to him
meant liberty to be himself, and thus the typical representative of the English eighteenth-century culture is a sturdy
individualist and conservative like Dr Johnson, who had
his roots deep in the national soil and the national tradition. Above all, the religious life of the people was still
strong, and received a fresh impetus from the great
Wesleyan movement, which is one of the central facts of
eighteenth-century history. While Voltaire was conducting
his campaign against religion among the upper classes on
the continent, the Wesleys and Whitefield were preaching
a revival of intense personal religion among the lower and
middle classes of England and the American colonies.
Their inspiration was derived from the Pietist movement of
Lutheran Germany, above all from the followers of Count
Zinzendorf, the Moravian Brethren, but the new doctrines
fell on a ground prepared by the Puritan tradition of the
seventeenth century, and acquired a thoroughly national
character. They appealed to just those classes which might
otherwise have afforded fruitful soil for the political agi-
tator and turned into religious channels the forces which on
the continent found an outlet in the revolutionary movement that was inspired by the social mysticism of
Rousseau. The religious conversion of the individual took
the place of the political revolution of society.

Nevertheless, the great intellectual movement that
originated with Newton and Locke did not cease or become
sterile in the country of its origin. But while in France it
became the source of a universal philosophy of Nature and
Humanity, in England it was averse to these ambitious
speculations and confined its activity to practical and
utilitarian objects. In this it was faithful to the Newtonian
tradition, with its hatred of hypothesis and its conception
of science as the means of assuring man's control and
utilization of the forces of nature. Hence, at the same time

that the French were attempting to reconstruct society on abstract principles, the English were carrying out a technical reconstruction of their economic life which was destined to have an even greater effect on the future of European civilization. The Industrial Revolution was only rendered possible by the new mathematical methods of Newton and his predecessors which had reduced mechanics to an exact science, and thus the mechanical civilization of the industrial age followed naturally upon the Newtonian conception of the mechanical order of nature. But it also required favourable social and economic conditions for its realization, and these also were found in the enterprising individualistic society of eighteenth-century England, in which the growth of trade supplied at once the necessary capital and an expanding market for a great industrial development. The invention of the steam engine, the development of the new coal-using metallurgy, and the application of mechanical power and finally of steam in the cotton industry, were the chief steps in the consequent Revolution which made England the workshop of the world and caused an enormous increase in the population. And this again acted as a stimulus upon agriculture, which was itself undergoing a revolution owing to the introduction of capital to farming.

At the same time, the economic policy of the nation was being transformed by the new science of political economy which has the same importance in the history of English thought as the movement of philosophic rationalism has in France. Though its founder, Adam Smith, derived considerable elements in his doctrine from contemporary French thought, it is essentially British in character and is the product of a Protestant and individualistic society. Its leading principles were the freedom of trade and industry, the harmfulness of all governmental regulation, and the desirability of free competition owing to the providential identity of private interests and the public advantage. Its later development was closely bound up with the philosophic radicalism of Bentham, and with the thoughts of Malthus and Ricardo, and it was the chief formative influence in the nineteenth-century liberalism of the Manchester School which triumphed in the Repeal of the Corn Laws.

This theoretic movement gave the Industrial Revolution its philosophy, and also had a powerful influence on practical politics and the transformation of social institutions in England. In spite of the enormous suffering that was caused by the unrestricted individualism and competition of the new industrial order, there was a vast increase of material power and prosperity, which made it possible for England to stand alone against Europe in the Napoleonic age. France was faced not only by the solid organization of the English agrarian state, but by the inexhaustible economic resources of the new industrial society. The continental blockade failed because the continent itself had become dependent on English trade and industry, while at the same time England's command of the sea enabled her to monopolize the extra-European markets at the expense of her continental rivals. Thus the defeat of Napoleon was a victory not so much of the old regime and the European forces of political reaction, but of the new economic society, which was as much a product of the new age as the French Revolution itself.

I I

The Revolution and the Modern World

THE history of the nineteenth century developed under the shadow of the French Revolution and the national liberal revolutions that followed it. A century of political, economic and social revolution, a century of world discovery, world conquest, and world exploitation, it was also the great age of capitalism; and yet saw too the rise of socialism and communism and their attack upon the foundations of capitalist society—St Simon, Fourier, Proudhon, Marx, Bakunin. When the century began, Jefferson was president in the United States, and George III was still King of England. When it ended Lenin already was planning the Russian Revolution.

The nineteenth century was also an age of immense scientific progress – both in thought and still more in the application of science to human life. This progress may seem elementary to us in the Atomic Age. Nevertheless, it was the nineteenth century that took the decisive steps on which everything else depended. For in 1800 mankind almost everywhere was living as it had always lived in the old round of peasant labourer and handicraft which had endured with so little change for thousands of years, while by 1900 the machine was everywhere, and at least the foundation of a world economy and a technological order had been laid. Thus western civilization in the nineteenth century was being transformed by two great movements of change which operated simultaneously from two different centres of origin. First there was the political revolution, which had its origin in the great French Revolution of

1789, and which was carried forward by the three later revolutions of 1830, 1848 and 1871 and which gradually ceased to be purely political and became social and socialist. And secondly there was the technological revolution, which began with the English Industrial Revolution at the end of the eighteenth century and gradually extended into continental Europe from the Atlantic with the coming of the railway and the factories and the new metallurgy and which gradually replaced the old agrarian economy of the peasant by the new urban industrial order.

In the past, cultural change, except in the religious sphere, was confined mainly to a small urban or aristocratic minority. Underneath this culturally active superstructure, the life of the masses went on almost unchanged. Civilization rested on an agrarian substructure, and the peasant majority followed its traditional patterns of life and used the same economic techniques century after century.

The technological revolution shifted the social and economic centre of gravity. The new urban industrial society became the dynamic centre of a world economy and it transformed the agrarian society to conform with its demands. The expansion of mechanized industrial production stimulated the demand for raw materials and ultimately led to the mechanization of agriculture.

This relation between the new urban mechanized culture and the old peasant economy is paralleled by that between the new culture and the non-European societies which were regarded as sources of raw material and which were profoundly changed by the stimuli and pressures of the western market.

Thus the new technological order produced profound social changes. The sudden change in the internal balance of power and the vast increase in wealth and opportunity set up a process of intense competition and social tension between individuals, classes and states.

The triumph of technology was the fruit of the scientific progress that had taken place in western Europe since the Renaissance. It had followed two different lines of development – the mathematical tradition of the great continental scientific thinkers from Galileo and Descartes and Leibniz to Lagrange and Laplace and Euler, and the experimental empiricism of the school of Francis Bacon and the Royal Society and Locke in England. But both these traditions have their roots in the Oxford School of the thirteenth century with Grosseteste and Roger Bacon and both came together in the modern technological tradition.

It was not, however, until this tradition was adopted and applied by the enterprise and invention of the new middle classes, especially the Protestant middle class in eighteenth-century England, that the immense economic and social effects of scientific technology were realized. A typical example of the forces that collaborated in the movement is to be seen in Watt's invention of the steam engine. This would have been impossible without the enlightened support of the men of science at Glasgow University with whom he worked. But it did not succeed without the further support of a dynamic and farsighted man of business – Matthew Boulton of Birmingham.

The movement as a whole was far from materialistic in spirit. The scientists were inspired by the Christian – Platonist conception of an intelligible world order which could be interpreted or translated in mathematical terms. The men of business were inspired by the Puritan conception of industry and enterprise as moral ideals. And the two were brought together by the liberal idealism of economic philosophers like Adam Smith, who believed that the freedom of trade and knowledge and industry would inevitably serve to increase the wealth of nations and the happiness of mankind. In reality, however, the application of science to life by technology meant a vast expansion of wealth and power which broke down the traditional social standards and undermined the traditional moral values. It was like a gold rush in which success fell to the strongest and the most unscrupulous and in which the weak went to the wall.

The age of technology, which was based on the application of science to life, should theoretically have led to the reorganization of the world by scientific intelligence on humane and liberal principles for the common good. Actually it became an age of confusion and disorder, of economic exploitation and social revolution, of scepticism and materialism. Never in the whole course of history have the forces of human stupidity, greed and selfishness manifested themselves on such a vast scale. Consequently, it is not surprising that all those who were aware of the traditional values of western culture should have reacted against the evil of the new age. As Burke and André Chénier and de Maistre reacted against the excesses of the French Revolution, so Carlyle and Ruskin reacted against the Industrial Revolution, while representatives of the Christian tradition revolted against the new dogmatism of the scientists and the materialism of the new industrial society.

On the whole, the Church was on the side of the conservatives, not only because the old order was officially and professedly a Christian one, but even more because the revolutionary changes of the new age seemed to be subverting the foundations of moral and social order and producing a state of disorder and disintegration.

On the other hand, the scientists and the technologists tended on the whole to support the liberal ideology, because they were conscious of the hostility of the vested interests of the old order and the intolerance of the political and religious authorities as the main obstacles to the progress of modern civilization.

Consequently, there was a conflict between Christian culture and liberal culture, and a corresponding alliance between Christianity and the vested interests of the old order, on the one hand, and between liberalism and the selfish appetites of the bourgeoisie and the revolutionary claims of the proletariat on the other. Yet neither of these alliances was sufficiently stable to provide a common ground on which western culture could be reunited. The whole period from the French Revolution to the present day has been characterized by a continual struggle between

conflicting ideologies; and the periods of relative
stabilization – by Napoleon after the French Revolution, by
Victorian liberalism in the mid-nineteenth century, and by
capitalist imperialism under the second German empire –
have all been compromises or temporary truces between
two periods of conflict.

The dominant ideology of the nineteenth century was
undoubtedly liberalism: it was the typical creed of the
bourgeoisie; of the new industrial and commercial interests
which sought to abolish all restrictions on the free play of
economic forces; of the political reformers, who advocated
constitutional government, personal liberty, and the abolition of feudal traditions, class privileges, and all forms of
arbitrary or authoritarian power; finally, it was the creed
of the intelligentsia, who were the champions of nationalism, freedom of thought, and the freedom of the press.

Yet in spite of their common traits, European liberalism was profoundly divided. French and indeed continental
liberalism was inspired by the tradition of the French
Revolution and was usually anti-clerical and often anti-
religious, whereas English liberalism drew much of its
strength from the support of the Nonconformists, and its
leaders, like John Bright and Gladstone, were often men of
strong religious convictions. Moreover the issue was complicated by the nationalist movement, which tended to
identify itself with liberalism in Italy and eastern Europe,
while in the west and north of Europe it tended to ally
itself with conservatism.

Finally, the movement of political revolution which
had begun by being liberal and national gradually evolved
in the direction of social revolution and a new socialist
ideology which was hostile to the bourgeoisie and to the
liberal constitutional state. In 1848 liberals and socialists
fought together on the same side of the barricades, but by
1871 they fought on opposite sides, so that Thiers, the old
leader of the liberals, became the merciless suppressor of
the Commune.

Socialism owed its strength not only to its support of
the claims of the workers against the middle classes, but

even more because it realized from the beginning the social implications of the technological revolution. This was due not to Marx but to the St Simonians who were not utopians of the type of Fourier and Cabet but rather technological idealists who believed that all social ills could be cured by a reorganization of society by the scientists, who were the modern representatives of the spiritual power, and the industrialists, who now represented the temporal power. These two powers were to be co-ordinated by their common allegiance to the principles of the new religion, which was a kind of rationalized, humanitarian version of Christianity, and was to form the basis of the new system of universal education which the St Simonians regarded as a necessary condition of the new social organization.

St Simonianism had an immense ideological influence not only in France but in Germany and Russia and even in England (through John Stuart Mill), but as a political movement it was a complete failure, largely owing to its conservative and religious tendencies. Socialism owed its world importance to its revolutionary character, and it was the Marxian combination of the ideology of dialectical materialism with the politics of communist revolution and class war and the techniques of revolutionary propaganda and party organization, that ultimately gained the support of the revolutionary intelligentsia and conquered in Russia and eastern Europe.

For during the latter part of the nineteenth century the spirit of western culture had changed, and the age was one of materialism alike in thought and in action. The new biological theories of evolution and natural selection were commonly interpreted in a way that justified the struggle for existence between states and classes and the survival of the 'fittest' or the most successful. Crude theories of racial and national superiority became popular. The liberal idealism that had inspired Adam Smith and the free trade movement gave way to a fiercely competitive economic nationalism and a colonial imperialism which reached its climax in the 'scramble for Africa' during the last twenty years of the nineteenth century. And while the international policies of the ruling classes were inspired by imperialism, nationalism and militarism, the opposing forces of revolutionary change likewise abandoned the ideals of their eighteenth-century and early nineteenth-century predecessors and turned to power politics and the use of force, whether they were communists, anarchists or nihilists.

Perhaps the most original and powerful writer of the later nineteenth century, Friedrich Nietzsche, is the greatest representative of the extreme tendencies of the age. He announced the passing of the two thousand years during which Europe had been dominated by Christian and humanist values and the necessity of an assertion of the Will to Power which transcends good and evil and which will eventually create a new type of superhumanity.

Under these circumstances it must seem remarkable that Europe in the last decades of the nineteenth century enjoyed an interval of exceptional peace and prosperity. The fact is that the common man knew nothing of the demonic forces that were agitating the depths of the European consciousness. All over Europe men were hard at work building new industries and creating a new pattern of urban life. It was the golden age of the *rentier*, the shop-keeper and the commercial traveller – an age whose spirit is represented by writers like Mark Twain, Rudyard Kipling and H. G. Wells rather than by Nietzsche and Strindberg.

The main cause of the defeat of liberalism in the later nineteenth century, however, was the alliance between the nationalist movement and the conservative state which created the German empire in 1870-1 and was followed by the period of intense national rivalries and colonial expansion which culminated in the First World War. The German empire owed its strength to the way in which it had harnessed modern technology and industry in the service of military and political power. Bismarck's Germany was the forerunner both of the totalitarian state and the welfare state, though it retained some links with the past, through the Christian conservatives on the one side and the national liberals on the other.

But after the First World War these traditional elements disappeared and the west was faced by two rival forces of totalitarianism, both of which were fully conscious of the importance of technology as the source of power, and of the possibility of applying new techniques of social and psychological control to eliminate ideological differences and to create a total state of unanimity, uniformity and unity.

For although parliamentary democracy and internationalism were nominally triumphant by the end of the First World War, a formidable accumulation of revolutionary forces had been building up which threatened their very existence. In addition to the revolutionary appeal of the Comintern, which had been launched by Lenin in 1919, and to the resentment and unrest of the German nationalists, who could not acquiesce in defeat, a new centre of disturbance had arisen in 1922 among the allies themselves. This was Italian fascism, which was the typical product of the anti-liberal tendencies which had developed in the later nineteenth century – the militant nationalism of D'Annunzio, the futurism of Marinetti, and the cult of violence and direct action expounded by Georges Sorel in 1906. The importance of fascism lay not so much in its effect on Italy as in the outlet it provided for all those subversive elements which rejected communism and yet demanded a revolutionary solution for their problems. The economic world depression of 1929 and the following years gave these forces their opportunity.

In Germany, above all, where the economic depression was exceptionally severe, fascism in its national socialist form was accepted with fanatical determination. It soon became evident that the totalitarian state was not the 'stunt' of an Italian demagogue, but a terrible reality which was capable of destroying the whole traditional order of European culture. Indeed, the 'New Order' inaugurated by the national socialist regime went far to fulfil Nietzsche's forecast concerning European nihilism, for though Adolf Hitler was very unlike the superman of Nietzsche's dreams, he was in fact the embodiment of a will to power which ignored good and evil and trampled under foot human rights and national liberties.

When this revolt against the whole Christian and humanist tradition of Europe merged in a Second World War which was even more total than the first, the destruction of Europe seemed imminent, and was only averted at immense material and moral cost. For the destruction of one form of totalitarianism involved the strengthening of the other, so that the fall of Hitler meant the triumph of Stalin and the advance of the communist world empire into the very heart of Europe.

Consequently, the end of the Second World War could not result, like the First World War, in a European settlement and the re-establishment of the hegemony of western Europe. The establishment of the United Nations at San Francisco in 1945, unlike the League of Nations, was essentially a non-European settlement which gave western Europe seven votes out of fifty and shifted the centres of world power eastwards to Moscow and westwards to Washington. The European society of states, which even fifty years ago was still the focus of world power and the leader of world civilization, had become a truncated fragment too small and too weak to exist without the military protection and the economic aid of the United States.

For meanwhile the balance of world power had been changed also by the emergence of a new centre of technological organization and industrial power outside Europe. In America western science and technology were free to develop on a continental scale undisturbed by the political and ideological conflicts of Europe, and the new western society was a technological one from the beginning, since it owed its very existence to the world market and the new forms of transport and communication – the steamship, the railway and the telegraph.

It is true that it had its own internal social conflict which culminated in the Civil War, but the war actually stimulated industrial production, and in the generation that followed the war the expansion of American industrialism created a system of concentrated economic power based on wider foundations than anything that existed elsewhere. But it was impossible for this technological power system to maintain its isolation from world politics. When the age of the world wars arrived, America was bound to intervene decisively. The fact that it was based on, or at least coexisted with, a liberal democratic ideology, made it the predestined enemy of the new totalitarian powers and the natural ally of the surviving free states in Europe – Britain, France, Holland and the Scandinavian states, as well as of the central European Jews who were the chief victims of the national socialist movement.

The intervention of the United States in the two World Wars (and especially the Second), stimulated the progress of technology within America, and its influence elsewhere, so that today the western version of the technological order is generally regarded as an American order and has become associated with the American democratic ideology, though in fact the latter had a different origin, since it was originally developed in the pre-technological age in an agrarian environment. The agrarian democracy of the age of Jefferson was transformed first by Jackson and later, more fundamentally, by the mass immigration from Europe in the second half of the nineteenth century, which prepared the way for the development of mass democracy.

The defeat of national socialism in the Second World War by the alliance of Soviet communism with American and British democracy has left the modern world divided between two opposing ideologies and political systems. Of these, the communist world, which now extends from the Baltic and the Adriatic to the Pacific, forms a single totalitarian power system and it also forms a united area for technological and industrial planning. The western world, on the other hand, is essentially pluralist and multiform in political power, in ideology, and in industrial and technological planning. Nor it is coextensive with the noncommunist world, for the countries of southern Asia and

Africa, which are technologically more backward than
either the communist or the western societies, tend to be
politically neutralist, and are a source of weakness rather
than of strength to the military power of the western
world. The ideological diversity of the modern western
world since 1945 resembles that of Europe in the nineteenth century.

There are Christians and rationalists, liberals and
conservatives, socialists and individualists, nationalists and
internationalists. This ideological division and conflict is a
source of weakness in so far as it provides a series of
opportunities for the totalitarian powers to apply their
techniques of disintegration, just as they do in the case of
the conflicts of political interest between the different
western states.

On the other hand, it is a source of strength in so far
as it is a necessary condition for the preservation of
freedom and the development of the different independent
aspects of western culture. But the survival of western
culture demands unity as well as freedom, and the great
problem of our time is how these two essentials are to be
reconciled.

For in the first place the progress of technology
demands a certain degree of international co-operation and
internal social unity if the work of organizing and integrat-
ing the material and human resources of the world is to be
carried on. In the long run the power of the west to
withstand the pressure of the communist totalitarian tech-
nocracy depends not so much on its military power as on
its cultural leadership and its scientific and technological
efficiency. But technological efficiency is not enough. Even
the totalitarian powers which are professedly materialist
owe their power not merely to force, but to their faith in
their ideology and their ethical values. And a free society
requires a higher degree of spiritual unity than a totalitarian one. Hence the spiritual integration of western
culture is essential to its temporal survival.

In what way Christianity can contribute to this work
of spiritual integration is not at present obvious, but no

historian can regard it as irrelevant that Christianity remains by far the strongest religious element in western culture, and however far the process of secularization has gone, the influence of Christianity on culture, in ethics, in education, in literature and in social action is still strong.

Consequently it is to Christianity that western culture must look for leadership and help in restoring the moral and spiritual unity of our civilization. If it fails to do so, it means either the failure of Christianity or the condemnation of modern civilization.

BIBLIOGRAPHY

This bibliography, though incomplete, shows that the author gave first place to contemporary journals and memoirs, from Mallet du Pan, who died in 1800, to witness who survived late into the 19th century. Clearly he intended a history of ideas, of its nature unaffected by more recent work on the society and economy of the age.

Alger, J. G., *Englishmen in the French Revolution*, London, 1889
Aulard, F. A., *L'Eloquence Parlementaire pendant la Révolution*, Paris, 1882
Aulard, F. A., *La Société des Jacobins*, Paris, 1889
Avenel, G., *A. Cloots, l'Orateur du genre Humain*, 2 vols, Paris, 1865
Babeau, A., *L'Ecole du Village pendant la Révolution*, Paris, 1881
Babeuf Conspiracy, 14 vols of tracts in British Museum
Barbaroux, C. J. M., *Mémoires*, Paris, 1827
Barbe-Marbois, F. de, *Journal d'un déporté*, 2 vols. Brussels, 1835
Barras, Comte P. F. Z. N. de, *Mémoires*, 4 vols, Paris, 1895-6
Bertrand de Moleville, *Mémoires Particulières*, 2 vols, Paris, 1816
Berville, St A et Barrière, *Mémoires pour servir . . .* 68 vols. Paris, 1821-8
Besenval, Baron P. V. de, *Mémoires*, 2 vols, Paris, 1821
Billaud-Varenne, *Curiosités révolutionnaires. Mémoires*, Paris, 1893
Blake, William, *Jerusalem*, 1804
Bougeart, A., *Marat, l'Ami du peuple*, 2 vols, Paris, 1865
Bradford, W., *History of the Plymouth Plantation*, ed. C. Deane, Boston, 1856
Brandes, Georg, *The Romantic Movement in Germany*, Copenhagen, 1873
Brinton, Prof., *The Jacobins*, New York, 1930
Bruggemann F., *Was Weltbild der deutschen AufKlärung*, Leipzig, 1930
Buchèz et Roux, *Histoire Parlementaire de la Révolution francaise*, Paris, 1834-8
Burke, Edmund, *Thoughts on the Prospect of a Regicide Peace*, London, 1796
Buzot, F. N. L., *Mémoires sur la Révolution francaise*, Paris, 1828
Carnot, Comte L. N. M., *Mémoires Historiques et Militaires sur Carnot*, Paris, 1824
Carnot, Comte L. N. M., *Réponse au Rapport fait sur la Conjuration du 18 fructidor*, London, 1799
Chuquet, A., *La Jaunesse de Napoléon*, Toulon, Paris, 1899
Cloquet, J. G., *Souvenirs sur la vie privée de Lafayette*, Paris, 1836

Coleridge, S. T., *Biographia Literaria*, 1817
Coleridge, S. T., *Essays on his own Times*, 3 vols, London, 1850
Comparative display of British Opinions on the French Revolution, 3 vols, London, 1811
Costa de Beauregard, A. Marquis, *Recollections*, 2 vols, London, 1877
Cretineau-Joly, J. A. M., *L'Eglise en face de la Révolution*, 2 vols, Paris, 1859
Currie, W., *Memoirs of Dr Currie*, 2 vols, London, 1831
Czartoryski, A. J., *Memoirs*, 2 vols, London, 1888
Dauban, C. A., *La Démogogie a Paris en 1794 et en 1795*, Paris, 1869
Daudet, E., *Histoire des Conspirations Royalistes du Midi sous la Révolution, 1790-3*, Paris, 1881
Daunou, P. C. F., *Mémoires*, Paris, 1846
Dejob, C., *Mme de Stael et l'Italie*, Paris, 1890
Descostes, F., *Joseph de Maistre pendant la Révolution francaise*, Tours, 1895
Dufourcq, A., *Le régime Jacobin Italie*, Paris, 1900
Dumas Davy de la Pailleterie, A., *I Borboni di Napoli*, 10 vols, Naples, 1862-3
Espinas, A., *La philosophie sociale du xviii siecle et la Révolution*, Paris, 1891
Fauche Borel, L., *Mémoires*, 4 vols, Paris, 1829
Ferrieres, C. E. Marquis de, *Mémoires*, 3 vols, Paris, 1821
Fersen, Count H. A. von, *Le Comte de Fersen et la cour de France*, 2 vols, Paris, 1877-8
Fitzmaurice, Lord E., *Life of Lord Shelburne*, London, 1876
Forneron, H., *Histoire des Emigrés*, 2 vols, Paris, 1884
Fortescue, J. B., MSS of The Dropmore Papers, 3 vols, London, 1892
Gohier, L. J., *Mémoires*, 2 vols, Paris, 1824
Goncourt, E. et J. de, *Histoire de la Société francaise pendant la Révolution*, Paris, 1889
Goyau, G., *La Pensée religieuse de J. de Maistre*, Paris, 1921
Granier de Cassagnac, A., *Histoire des Causes de la Révolution francaise de 1789*, Paris, 1850
Groethuysen, *Origine de l'esprit Bourgeois en France*, Paris, 1927
Hamel, E., *Histoire de Saint-Just*, Brussels, 1860
Holcroft, T., *Memoirs*, 3 vols, London, 1816
Huffer, H., *Der Rastatter Congress*, Bonn, 1896
Janet, P., *La Philosophie de la Révolution francaise*, Paris, 1892
Jaurès, J., *Histoire Socialiste de la Révolution francaise*, ed. Mathiez, Paris, 1922-4
Jordan, C., *Camille Jordan, Deputé du Rhone, à ses commettans sur la révolution du 18 fructidor*, Paris, 1797
Jung, H. F. T., *Bonaparte et son Temps (1769-99)*, 3 vols, Paris, 1885
Kent, C., *The English Radicals*, London, 1899
Knight, C., *Autobiography*, London, 1861
Lafayette, Marquis de, *Mémoires et correspondance du general Lafayette*, 6 vols, Paris, 1837-8
Lally-Tollendal, Comte T. G. de, *Défense des Emigrés francais*, Paris, 1797
Lanfrey, P., *L'église et les philosophes au XVIII siecle*, Paris, 1879
Lanson, G., *Voltaire*, Paris, 1906

Lanzac de Laborie, L. de, *Jean-Joseph Mounier*, Paris, 1887

La Revellière de Lepeaux, L. M. de, *Mémoires*, 3 vols, Paris, 1895

Larivière, C. de, *Catherine II et la Révolution francaise*, Paris, 1895

Lavisse, E., *Histoire de France*, Paris, 1920-22

Lebon, A., *L'Angleterre et l'Emigration francaise*, Paris, 1882

Legrand, L., *La Révolution francaise en Hollande*, Paris, 1895

Lenotre, G., *Vieilles maisons, Vieux papiers*, Paris, 1908

Lescure, M. F. A. de, *Rivarol et la Société pendant la Révolution et l'Emigration*, Paris, 1883

Levae, A., *Les Jacobins de Bruxelles*, Brussels, 1846

Lichtenberger, A., *Le Socialisme utopique*, Oswald, Paris, 1898

Ligne, C. J., Prince de, *Mémoires*, Paris, 1860

Lomenie, L. de, *Beaumarchais et son temps*, Paris, 1856.

Lynedoch, Lord (Col. T. Graham), *Memoir of*, by J. M. Graham, Edinburgh, 1847

Mackintosh, R., *Life of Sir J. Mackintosh*, 2 vols, London, 1835

Madden, R., *The United Irishmen*, 7 vols, London, 1842-6

Maistre, J., Comte de, *Considérations sur la France, 1797*, Oeuvres, Lyon, 1884-7

Mallet, B., *Mallet du Pan and the French Revolution*, London, 1902

Mallet du Pan, J. F., *Mercure Britannique*, London, 1798-1800

Mallet du Pan, J. F., *Correspondance inédite avec la Cour de Vienne (1794-8)*, 2 vols, Paris, 1884

Mallet du Pan, J. F., *La Révolution francaise vue de L'etranger*, ed. Descostes, Paris, 1897

Malmesbury, J. H., Earl of, *Diaries and Correspondence*, 4 vols, London, 1884.

Malouet, Baron P. V. de, *Mémoires*, 2 vols, Paris, 1874

Marat, J. P., *Oeuvres*, ed. Vermorel, Paris, 1869

Marmont, A. F. L., Viesse de, Marshal, *Mémoires*, 9 vols, Paris, 1857

Masson, F., *Les Diplomates de la Révolution*, Paris, 1882

Mehring, F., *Geschichte der Deutschen Sozialdemokratie I*, Stuttgart, 1897

Meister, J. H., *Souvenirs de mon dernier voyage à Paris*, Paris, 1797

Mercy-Argenteau, Comte F. de, *Correspondance secrète avec l'Impératrice Marie-Thérèse*, 3 vols, Paris, 1875

Mercy-Argenteau, Comte F. de, *Correspondance secrète avec l'Empereur Joseph II et le Prince de Kaunitz*, 3 vols, Paris, 1889-91

Miles, W., *Correspondence on the French Revolution*, 2 vols, London, 1890

Mirabeau, G. H. R., Comte de, *Correspondance avec le Comte de la Marck*, ed. Bacourt, 3 vols, Paris, 1851

Moody, C. L., *A sketch of modern France ...*, London, 1798

Moore, Dr J., *View of the causes and progress of the French Revolution*, 2 vols, London, 1795

Mounier, J. J., *De l'influence attribuée aux Philosophes ... sur la Révolution de France*, Paris, 1822

Muralt, C. von, *Hans von Reinhard*, Zurich, 1838

Nippold, F., *Handbuch der neuesten Kirchengeschichte*, Berlin, 1889

Paine, Thomas, *Common Sense*, 2nd ed., 1776

Paine, Thomas, *Rights of Man*, 1791

Paul, C. Kegan, *William Godwin*, 2 vols, London, 1876

Pepe, General G., *Memorie*, Paris, 1847

Perthes, F., *Memoirs,* vol 1, 2 vols, London, 1857

Pingaud, L., *Les Francais en Russie et les Russes en France,* Paris, 1886

Pontecoulant, L. G., Comte de, *Souvenirs historiques et parlementaires,* 4 vols, Paris, 1861-5

Puisaye, Comte J. G. de, *Mémoires,* 6 vols, London, 1803-8

Rambaud, A. N., *Les Francais sur le Rhin,* 1790-1804, Paris, 1873

Ramel, J. P., *Journal,* Hamburg, 1799. Eng. trans., London, 1799

Reinhard, Comte C. F. de, *Lettres à ma Mere,* Paris, 1901

Révolution francaise, la; *Revue Historique,* Paris, 1910 etc.

Robison, J., *Proofs of a Conspiracy against all the Religions and Governments of Europe,* Edinburgh, 1797

Roederer, Comte P. L., *Oeuvres,* 8 vols, Paris, 1853-9

Roland, Mme., *Lettres,* ed. C. Perroud, Paris, 1900

Rose, G., *Diaries and Correspondence,* 2 vols, London, 1860

Rousseau, J. J., *Lettres écrites de la montagne,* 1765

Saint-Just, *Fragmens sur les institutions républicaines,* Paris, 1831

Schlegel, F., *Neue Philosophische Schriften,* Frankfurt, 1935

Schmidt, W. A., *Tableaux de la Révolution francaise,* 3 vols, Leipzig, 1867-71

Segur, Comte P. P. de, *Mémoires d'un aide-de-camp de Napoléon,* 3 vols, Paris, 1894-5

Smith, E., *The English Jacobins,* London, 1881

Sombart, W., *Der proletarische Sozialismus,* Jena, 1924

Sorel, A., *L'Europe et la Revolution francaise,* Paris, 1885-1903

Stael, Mme de, *Considérations sur les principaux événements de la Révolution,* London, 1819

Steffens, H., *Was ich erlebte,* 10 vols (vols I-II), Breslau, 1840-4

Stephenson, N. W., *A History of the American People,* New York, 1934

Stern, A., *Das Leben Mirabeaus,* 2 vols, Berlin, 1889

Swift, Jonathan, *An Argument . . .,* 1708

Talleyrand-Périgord, C. M. de, Prince, *Mémoires,* 5 vols, Paris, 1891-2

Thelwall, Mrs, *Life of John Thelwall,* London, 1837

Thibaudeau, Comte A. C., *Mémoires, 1765-92,* Paris, 1875

Thiébault, Baron D., General, *Mémoires,* 5 vols, Paris, 1893-5

Thompson, J. M., *Robespierre,* Oxford, 1935

Tone, T. Wolfe, *Autobiography,* ed. R. B. O'Brien, 2 vols, London, 1893

Tournois, *Histoire du parti d'Orléans . . .,* 2 vols, Paris, 1842

Turreau de Garambouville, Baron L. M., *Mémoires . . . de la guerre de la Vendée,* Paris, 1824

Vaudreuil, Comte H. H. F., Rigaud de, *Correspondance,* Paris, 1889

Viatte, M., *Les sources occultes du romantisme,* Paris, 1928

Vieux Cordelier, le, *Journal redigé par Camille Desmoulins,* 7 nos., Paris, 1793-4

Vivenot, A. von, *Vertrauliche Briefe von Thugut,* 2 vols, Vienna, 1872,

Wakefield, G., *Memoirs,* 2 vols, London, 1804

Watson, R., *Anecdotes,* 2 vols, London, 1816

Williams, G., *History of the Liverpool Privateers,* London, 1897

Windham, W., *Diary,* London, 1886.

INDEX